1250

BEN NICHOLSON

paintings
reliefs
drawings

painting (2 circles) *1945*   collection Margaret Gardiner

BEN NICHOLSON

paintings

reliefs

drawings

volume I

with an introduction by HERBERT READ

Lund Humphries London

first edition 1948

reprinted 1955 — work from 1911 to 1948 volume 1

made and printed in Great Britain by

PERCY LUND HUMPHRIES AND COMPANY LIMITED LONDON AND BRADFORD

CONTENTS

list of plates   7

list of owners   11

introduction by Herbert Read   13

bibliography   21

biographical note   22

notes on "abstract" art by Ben Nicholson   23

résumé in French of introduction   29

translation in French of notes on "abstract" art   31

plates   1 to 203

the publishers wish to acknowledge with gratitude the assistance that has been given throughout by Thurairajah Tambimuttu of Messrs. Poetry London Ltd.: it was he who originally conceived the idea of this publication

this volume has been supervised and laid out by the artist, Ben Nicholson

the photographs of work produced from (approximately) 1924–34 were taken by Paul Laib, London; from 1934–39 by Barbara Hepworth; from 1939–48 by "Studio St. Ives", Cornwall

the following minor revisions of plates occur in this volume as compared with the First Edition

new plates have been substituted for plates 8, 52, 120, 165 and 175, and plate 165 replaces the original frontispiece

plate 119 now appears in monochrome instead of in full colour

the following five new plates have been added to this edition: 63a, 63b, 150a, 150b and 150c

LIST OF PLATES

frontispiece: painting (2 circles) 1945 *oil on board (19″ × 18″)*

1 striped jug, 1911: *oil on canvas (first painting), c. 20″ × 26″*

2 still life (*Balearic Islands*), 1925: *oil on canvas, c. 24″ × 24″*

3 Bré Ticino, 1921: *pencil on paper, 8½″ × 14″*

4 still life, Villa Capriccio, Castagnola, 1921–22: *oil on canvas, 24½″ × 29½″*

5 coast of Spain (*destroyed*) 1922–23: *oil on board, c. 14″ × 18″*

6 Cortivallo, Lugano, 1921: *oil on board, 18″ × 24″*

7 bottle and goblet, c. 1924: *oil on board, 11″ × 16″*

8 goblet and two pears, 1924

9 painting (*trout*), 1924: *oil on canvas, 22″ × 23″*

10 painting (*destroyed*), c. 1923–24: *oil on board, c. 16″ × 20″*

11 still life (*destroyed*), 1926: *oil on canvas, c. 22″ × 23″*

12 still life with fruit (*version 1*), 1926: *oil on canvas, 24″ × 23½″*

13 still life (*L.L.*), 1926: *oil on canvas, c. 30″ × 22″*

14 flowers, c. 1927: *oil on canvas, 14¾″ × 15¼″*

15 still life with knife and lemon, 1927: *oil on canvas, 36″ × 48″*

16† still life with fruit, 1927: *oil on canvas, 24½″ × 30¼″*

17† Le Quotidien, 1934: *oil on canvas, 15¾″ × 20⅜″*

18 still life, 1930: *oil on board, c. 7½″ × 16″*

19† prince and princess, 1932: *oil on board, 18″ × 12″*

20 still life with pear, 1931–32: *oil on canvas, 12½″ × 31½″*

21† pomegranate, 1929: *oil on canvas, 18¾″ × 22½″*

22† prince and princess, 1930: *oil on board, 5¼″ × 7¼″*

23 Cumbrian farm (*destroyed*), c. 1929: *oil on canvas, c. 20″ × 24″*

24 Cornish port, c. 1930: *oil on board, 8½″ × 13½″*

25 Cumbrian landscape, c. 1928: *oil on canvas, c. 18¼″ × 22¼″*

26 apples, c. 1927: *oil on canvas, 17¾″ × 27″*

27 Porthmeor beach, St. Ives, 1928: *oil on canvas, 36″ × 48″*

28 still life, c. 1927: *oil on board, c. 19¼″ × 24″*

29 flowers, c. 1924–25: *pencil and crayon on paper, 8¾″ × 11¼″*

30 breakfast table, Banks Head—Villa Capriccio, c. 1928: *pencil on paper, 13½″ × 16⅞″*

31 Cumbrian landscape (*version 1*), 1928: *oil on canvas, 22″ × 24″*

32 Pill Creek, Cornwall, 1928: *oil and pencil on canvas, 19″ × 24″*

33 profile (*Venetian red*), 1932: *oil on canvas, c. 50″ × 36″*

34† still life, 1932: *oil on canvas, 13″ × 16″*

35† still life, 1929–35: *oil and pencil on canvas, 26″ × 32″*

36† still life (*Mediterranean*), 1933: *oil on board, 11″ × 15½″*

37 St. Remy, Provence, 1932: *pencil on paper, 12″ × 15″*

38 two diamonds, 1929: *oil on board, 16″ × 22″*

39 Cumbrian landscape (*version 2*), 1928: *oil on canvas, 18″ × 24″*

40 frostbound (*Cumberland*), c. 1927–28: *oil on canvas, 20″ × 24″*

41 girl in mirror, 1933: *oil on board, 23½″ × 23½″*

42 still life, 1933–35: *oil on board, 20″ × 24″*

43 girl in mirror, 1932: *pencil on paper, 15″ × 12¼″*

44 girl in mirror, 1932: *pencil on paper, 15″ × 12¼″*

45 nude, 1932: *pencil on paper, 14¾″ × 12¼″*

46 Seine, Paris, c. 1932–33: *pencil on paper, 13¾″ × 18″*

47 Kate, Paris, c. 1933: *pencil on paper, 13½″ × 16⅞″*

48 Journal de Rouen, 1932: *oil on canvas, c. 28″ × 14″*

49 guitar, 1933: *oil on canvas, c. 27″ × 22″*

50 painting, 1933: *oil on board, c. 14″ × 25″*

51 Pont Royal, Paris, c. 1932–33: *pencil on paper, 13¼″ × 18″*

52 still life, 1932: *17¾″ × 23¾″*

53 St. Remy, Provence, 1933: *oil on board, 42″ × 36½″*

54 playing cards, 1932: *oil on board, 12¾″ × 16¾″*

55 painted relief (*first relief*), December, 1933: *oil on carved board, 21½″ × 10″*

56 six circles, 1933: *oil on carved board, 45″ × 22″*

57 guitar, 1933: *oil on board, 32¾″ × 7¾″*

58† Au Chat Botté, 1932: *oil on canvas, 36″ × 47¾″*

59† painting, 1933: *oil on canvas, 7⅞″ × 13⅞″*

60† act-drop curtain for Beethoven 7th Symphony ballet, 1934: *oil on board, 8⅞″ × 10¼″ : scale, 1″ to 8′*

61 sketch for 7th Symphony ballet, 1934: *oil on board, 5⅜″ × 7½″*

62 décor for 7th Symphony ballet, 4th movement, *1939 version*: *oil on carved board, 15¼″ × 19½″*

63 Auberge de la Sole Dieppoise, 1932: *oil on board, 35½″ × 29½″*

63a two fishes (Rouen), 1932: *oil on canvas, 27″ × 30″*

63b two heads, 1932: *pencil on paper*

64 painting (*hibiscus*), 1933: *oil on board, 51½″ × 21½″*

65 painting, 1933: *oil on board, 29″ × 36″*

66 coin and musical instruments, 1933: *oil on board, 42″ × 48″*

67 project, 1934: *oil on board, 7″ × 6½″*

68 still life, 1934: *oil, 17½″ × 25⅜″*

69 white relief, 1934: *oil on carved board, 13¾″ × 24″*

70 relief, 1934: *oil on carved board, c. 24″ × 16″*

71 white relief, 1938: *oil and pencil on carved board, c. 7″ × 11″*

72† painting, 1937: *oil on canvas, 62″ × 78¾″*

73† painting (*version 1*), 1937: *oil on canvas, 10″ × 8″*

74† painting (*version 1*), 1938: *oil on canvas, 48½″ × 55½″*

75† painting, 1938: *oil on canvas, 27½″ × 35½″*

76 painting (*version 1*), 1942: *gouache, 14½″ × 20½″*

77 still life (*Bocquet*), 1932: *oil on wooden signboard, 25½″ × 20″*

78 still life (*Italian*), 1934: *oil on canvas, 12½″ × 27½″*

79 white relief, 1934: *oil on carved board, 6″ × 8″*

80 white relief (*triplets*), October 2–34: *oil on carved board, 47½″ × 24″*

81 painting, 1935: *oil on canvas, 25″ × 36¾″*

82 painting (*Florentine ballet*), 1934: *oil on canvas, 14″ × 24″*

83 painting (*cadmium red, lemon and cerulean*), 1936: *oil on canvas, 69½″ × 42″*

84 white relief (*quai d'Auteuil*), 1935: *oil on carved board, 41″ × 46″*

85 painted relief (*plover's egg blue*), 1940: *oil on carved board, 18¼″ × 18¼″*

86† Towednack, 1943: *oil on board, 14¾″ × 18¾″*

87† painting (*milk and plain chocolate*), 1933: *oil on board, 53″ × 32″*

88 painting, 1933: *oil on board, c. 50″ × 24″*

89 painted relief, 1935: *oil on carved board, 44″ × 47″*

90 painting, 1935: *oil on canvas, 40″ × 41½″*

91 white relief, 1935: *oil on carved mahogany, 39″ × 65″*

92 white relief, 1936: *oil on carved board, 42″ × 53½″*

93 still life, 1933–35: *oil on board, 24″ × 30″*

94 still life (*Punch and Judy show*), 1932–37: *oil on canvas, 31″ × 37½″*

95 still life (*Greek landscape*), 1931–36: *oil on canvas, 26¾″ × 30″*

96 white relief, 1939: *oil on carved board, 30½″ × 29″*

97 painted relief (*version 1*), 1941: *oil on carved board, 31″ × 29″*

98 white relief (*version 1*), 1939: *oil on carved board, 42¾″ × 41″*

99 white relief 1938: *oil on carved board, c. 25″ × 25″*

100 painted relief, 1939: *oil on carved board, 41½″ × 38″*

101 Halse Town, 1939–41: *oil on board, 13″ × 16½″*

102 Halse Town, c. 1941: *pencil on paper*, $5\frac{1}{4}'' \times 7\frac{1}{8}''$

103 St. Ives rooftops (*version 2*), 1940: *oil on wood, c.* $13'' \times 17''$

104 still life, 1932–40: *oil on canvas*, $21\frac{1}{2}'' \times 26\frac{1}{4}''$

105 white relief, 1938: *oil on carved plywood, c.* $27'' \times 31''$

106† two forms (*version 8*), 1940–42: *gouache*, $36'' \times 35\frac{3}{4}''$

107† painting (*version 1*), 1943: *gouache*, $48'' \times 42''$

108 drawing (*version 1*), 1936: *oil and pencil on board*, $15'' \times 11\frac{3}{4}''$

109 Halse Town, 1939: *oil on board*, $12'' \times 15\frac{3}{4}''$

110 painting, 1937: *oil on canvas*, $24\frac{1}{2}'' \times 19\frac{1}{2}''$

111 St. Ives rooftops, 1940: *pencil on paper*, $10'' \times 17\frac{1}{4}''$

112 still life, 1945: *oil on canvas*, $18'' \times 19''$

113 St. Ives, 1940: *oil on board*, $12\frac{3}{4}'' \times 15\frac{3}{8}''$

114 painted relief (*version 1*), 1940: *oil on carved board*, $21'' \times 20''$

115 still life, 1930–42: *oil and pencil on canvas*, $18\frac{1}{2}'' \times 17\frac{3}{4}''$

116 painted relief (*version 1*), 1941: *oil on carved board*, $29'' \times 40''$

117 white relief, 1936: *oil on carved board*, $8'' \times 9\frac{1}{4}''$

118† painted relief (*version 1*), 1939: *oil on carved board*, $33'' \times 45''$

119 Higher Carnstabba farm, 1944: *oil on canvas*, $21\frac{1}{2}'' \times 21\frac{1}{2}''$

120 relief (1944)

121† playing cards, 1945: *oil on canvas*, $6\frac{1}{8}'' \times 9\frac{5}{8}''$

122† still life (*Chinese*), 1945: *oil and pencil on lino*, $16'' \times 16\frac{1}{4}''$

123† painted relief (*version 1*), 1943–44: *oil on carved board*, $33'' \times 40''$

124 fruit, 1944: *pencil on paper*, $9'' \times 12\frac{1}{2}''$

125 St. Ives rooftops *version 1*, 1940: *oil on wood, c.* $13'' \times 17''$

126 Cornish landscape (*Lelant*), c. 1940–41: *pencil on paper*, $12\frac{3}{4}'' \times 14\frac{3}{4}''$

127 project, 1941: *oil on carved board*, $9\frac{7}{8}'' \times 8\frac{3}{4}''$

128 Zennor, 1941: *pencil on paper*, $12\frac{3}{8}'' \times 6\frac{1}{8}''$

129 painted relief (*version 1*), 1941: *oil on carved board*, $28'' \times 55\frac{1}{2}''$

130 white relief (*version 1*), 1938: *oil on carved board*, $48'' \times 72''$

131 Mousehole, summer–47: *oil on board*, $15\frac{1}{2}'' \times 18\frac{3}{4}''$

132 St. Ives, 1943–45: *oil on canvas*, $15\frac{11}{16}'' \times 19\frac{1}{2}''$

133† still life, 1945: *oil and pencil on canvas*, $22\frac{1}{2}'' \times 21''$

134† playing cards, 1945: *oil and pencil on board*, $6\frac{1}{4}'' \times 8\frac{3}{4}''$

135† parrot's eye, 1945: *oil and pencil on board*, $7'' \times 9''$

136 three mugs, 1944: *oil and pencil on board*, $7'' \times 8\frac{1}{2}''$

137 project, 1942: *oil and pencil on board*, $5\frac{1}{4}'' \times 4\frac{1}{2}''$

138 playing cards, 1945: *oil on carved board*, $9\frac{1}{8}'' \times 11\frac{3}{4}''$

139 still life and port (*St. Ives*), 1943: *oil on canvas*, $14'' \times 18''$

140 still life (*Mount's Bay*), July 20–47: *oil on canvas*, $23\frac{3}{8}'' \times 10\frac{1}{8}''$

141 still life, 1945: *oil on canvas*, $24'' \times 14\frac{1}{4}''$

142 painting, 1943–44: *gouache*, $11\frac{5}{8}'' \times 9\frac{1}{16}''$

143 still life, 1945: *oil on canvas*, $13\frac{5}{8}'' \times 23\frac{3}{4}''$

144 still life and Cornish landscape, 1944: *oil on board*, $33'' \times 30''$

145 still life (*Fra Angelico*), 1946: *oil and pencil on board*, $9\frac{3}{4}'' \times 7\frac{1}{8}''$

146 Halse Town, 1942: *oil on lino*, $9\frac{4}{5}'' \times 12\frac{1}{2}''$

147 painted relief (*Arabian desert*), 1944–45: *oil on carved board*, $36'' \times 30''$

148 painted relief (*version 2*), 1943: *gouache on carved board, c.* $14\frac{1}{2}'' \times 18\frac{1}{2}''$

149 painted relief, 1943

150 goblets, 1947: *oil on board, c.* $9'' \times 8\frac{1}{2}''$

150a still life (*shop window*), 1946: *oil on canvas*

150b still life on table, 1947: *pencil on paper*

150c still life, June 16–47: *oil on canvas*, $15\frac{1}{2}'' \times 17\frac{1}{2}''$

151 Little Trevarrack, 1945: *oil on board*, $17\frac{1}{8}'' \times 13\frac{1}{4}''$

152 project, 1943: *oil on carved board*, $9\frac{3}{4}'' \times 12''$

153 still life, 1946: *oil on canvas*, $17\frac{1}{8}'' \times 13\frac{3}{4}''$

154 project, 1945: *oil and pencil on board*, $8'' \times 7\frac{5}{8}''$

155 two mugs, 1944: *oil on board*, $10'' \times 13\frac{5}{8}''$

156 Cornish landscape, summer–45: *pencil on paper*, $9\frac{3}{4}'' \times 14''$

157 Carbis Bay, summer–46: *pencil on paper,* $9'' \times 13\frac{7}{8}''$

158 still life, 1945: *oil on canvas,* $32\frac{5}{8}'' \times 25\frac{3}{4}''$

159 painting (*yellow on grey*), 1946: *oil and pencil on canvas,* $12\frac{1}{4}'' \times 16\frac{1}{2}''$

160 St. Ives, 1945: *oil on board,* $14\frac{5}{8}'' \times 17\frac{1}{8}''$

161 mug and goblets, 1947: *oil and pencil on board,* $9\frac{1}{2}'' \times 10\frac{1}{2}''$

162 Towednack, summer–46: *pencil on paper,* $9'' \times 14''$

163 still life, 1943–44: *oil on canvas,* $13\frac{5}{8}'' \times 23\frac{5}{8}''$

164† painting (*Arizona*), 1946: *oil and pencil on board,* $8\frac{5}{8}'' \times 11\frac{1}{8}''$

165 May 21–48 (*cat not under table*): *oil and pencil on canvas,* $42\frac{3}{4}'' \times 47\frac{3}{4}''$

166 painted relief, 1943: *oil on carved board,* $12'' \times 8\frac{1}{2}''$

167 Hayle estuary, May–46: *pencil on paper,* $9'' \times 13\frac{7}{8}''$

168 project (*green-brown*), February 13–47: *oil and pencil on board,* $11\frac{3}{8}'' \times 10\frac{7}{8}''$

169 still life (*Zennor Head*), 1946: *oil on canvas,* $29\frac{1}{4}'' \times 26\frac{1}{4}''$

170 painted relief 1944–45: *oil on carved board, c.* $28\frac{1}{2}'' \times 29''$

171 still life (*Lelant*), June 14–47: *oil and pencil on board,* $23'' \times 23\frac{1}{2}''$

172 project, 1946: *oil and pencil on board,* $10\frac{3}{4}'' \times 7\frac{1}{4}''$

173 still life (*Alice through looking-glass*), 1946: *oil and pencil on canvas,* $26\frac{7}{8}'' \times 29\frac{3}{4}''$

174 still life, 1947: *pencil on paper,* $15\frac{1}{4}'' \times 12\frac{3}{4}''$

175 Lelant, Cornwall, 1946: *oil on canvas,* $9'' \times 14''$

176 Portreath, summer–45: *pencil on paper,* $9\frac{3}{4}'' \times 14''$

177 Trendrine, summer–47: *pencil on paper,* $10\frac{7}{8}'' \times 13\frac{3}{4}''$

178 fives, February 12–47: *oil and pencil on board,* $7\frac{7}{8}'' \times 9\frac{1}{4}''$

179† still life (*spotted curtain*), March 14–47: *oil on board,* $23\frac{1}{2}'' \times 25\frac{1}{4}''$

180† still life (*poisonous green*), 1947: *oil on canvas,* $15'' \times 14\frac{1}{2}''$

181† Mousehole, November 11–47: *oil on canvas,* $20'' \times 24''$

182† Trevega, 1946: *oil on board,* $20'' \times 22\frac{1}{4}''$

183† project for two forms (*version I*), 1946–47: *oil on canvas,* $38'' \times 43''$

184† still life (*winter landscape*), 1946: *oil on canvas,* $23\frac{1}{2}'' \times 22\frac{3}{8}''$

185 painting (*version I*), 1944–45: *oil on canvas,* $35\frac{3}{4}'' \times 33\frac{1}{2}''$

186 still life (*Odyssey 2*), July 25–47: *oil on wood,* $21\frac{3}{8}'' \times 14\frac{5}{16}''$

187 Lelant, summer–47: *pencil on paper,* $9\frac{1}{8}'' \times 13\frac{7}{8}''$

188 still life, November 25–46: *oil on canvas,* $24\frac{1}{2}'' \times 19\frac{3}{4}''$

189 painting, 1945: *oil and pencil on canvas,* $13\frac{1}{8}'' \times 18\frac{1}{4}''$

190 foxy, June 15–47: *oil on board,* $7\frac{1}{8}'' \times 7\frac{3}{16}''$

191 still life (*cerulean*), 1946: *oil on canvas,* $24\frac{5}{8}'' \times 24\frac{1}{2}''$

192 still life (*oval theme*), July 8–47: *oil on canvas,* $24'' \times 20\frac{3}{8}''$

193 Newlyn, summer–47: *pencil on paper,* $9\frac{5}{8}'' \times 13\frac{7}{8}''$

194 Mousehole, summer–47: *pencil on paper,* $12\frac{3}{4}'' \times 18''$

195 painting (*yellow and violet on brown*), February 5–47: *oil on synthetic board,* $24'' \times 16\frac{3}{4}''$

196 Mount's Bay, summer–47: *pencil on paper,* $9'' \times 13\frac{3}{4}''$

197 project (*pyramid*), March–47: *oil on board,* $8\frac{1}{4}'' \times 8\frac{3}{8}''$

198† still life (*Odyssey I*), July 22–47: *oil on canvas,* $26\frac{1}{4}'' \times 21\frac{1}{4}''$

199† painted relief (*West Penwith*), November 23–46: *oil on carved board,* $20\frac{1}{2}'' \times 33''$

200† painting (*J.L.M.*), February 2–47: *oil and pencil on board,* $14\frac{3}{4}'' \times 12''$

201 Trendrine (2), December 13–47: *oil on canvas,* $15\frac{1}{8}'' \times 14\frac{5}{8}''$

202 still life (*brown and green*), November–47: *oil on board,* $18'' \times 23\frac{3}{4}''$

203 still life (*rhino*), March 13–47: *oil on canvas,* $23'' \times 23''$

---

note: dimensions always give the vertical measurement first; where several versions have been produced of one work the dimensions of the largest work only appear
c. means approximately
† colour plates

plate 71 is reproduced by courtesy of Polemic, *Plate 134 by* Horizon: *plate 71 was originally reproduced in* Focus 3: *plates 21, 22, 36, 58, 59, 106, 118, 122, 123, 133 and 135 are reproduced by courtesy of Penguin Books Ltd*

LIST OF OWNERS

Aberdeen Art Gallery
Adams, Miss Mary
Albright Gallery, Buffalo Museum,
   New York State, U.S.A.
Aldridge, John
Allen, R. F. F.
American University,
   Washington, U.S.A.
Anderson, Sir Colin
Antwerp, Musée Royal des Beaux-Arts
Archdale, Miss Ann
Archdale, James
Arts Council, The (2)
Astaldi, Mrs. Anna Maria, Italy
Atkinson, Fello
Ault, Lee (U.S.A.)

Baker Furniture Inc. (U.S.A.)
Baker, L. Y. (2)
Barnes, E. C. (2)
Barns-Graham, Miss W.
Barrett, W. P.
Barrow, Col. John (U.S.A.)
Bartos, Armand (U.S.A.)
Baxandall, David (2)
Baynes, Keith
Benenson, William
Bennett, Tim, the late
Bennitt, Mortimer, (3)
Benson, A. C., the late
Bentick, Lord
Berger, Miss Trude
Best, Alan
Birmingham City Art Gallery
Blanco-White, Mrs.
Bloc, André (France)
Bomford, H. J. P.
Bowyer, Gordon
Brash, Charles (N.Z.)
Brewer, Joseph (U.S.A.)
Brickell, A. W.
Brinckley, Goddard
Bristol City Art Gallery (2)
British Council, The (10)
Brown, Miss
Brown, Nicholas
Brumwell, J. R. M. (6)
Brussels, Musées Royaux des Beaux-
   Arts
Bunshaft, Gordon (U.S.A.)

Calder, Alexander (2) (U.S.A.)
Cameron, Roderick
Canadian National Gallery,
   Ottawa, Canada
Carola, Mme. Paola (France)
Carter, E. J.

Cast, G. D.
Catleugh, J .D. H. (3)
Cavaglieri, Mme. (France)
Cemlyn-Jones, C. W.
Chapman, Gilbert (U.S.A.)
Chermayeff, Serge (3) (U.S.A.)
Clark, Sir Kenneth (3)
Clutterbuck, Mrs. (2)
Coates, Wells
Contemporary Art Society (3)

Dannatt, Trevor
Davies, Mrs. Pat
Delville, E. (Belgium)
Derenberg, Mrs. Hedj and Carl (2)
Detroit Institute of Arts, U.S.A. (2)
Devine, Jerry (U.S.A.)
Diamond, Mrs. Hester and
   Harold, (2) (U.S.A.)
Dix, George E. (U.S.A.)
Dix, John C. W. (U.S.A.)
Drey, Miss Agnes
Ducrest, J. P. (France)
Duncan Phillips Gallery,
   Washington, U.S.A. (2)
Ducrest, J. P. (France)
Durlacher Brothers (U.S.A.)

Eates, Miss Margot (2)
Ede, H. S. (17)
Eden, The Hon. Mr. and Mrs. M.
Edinburgh College of Art
Elmhirst, Mrs. Dorothy, (3)
Erni, Hans (2)
Erskine, Hon. Robert
Evill, W. A.

Fader, Maxwell (U.S.A.)
Forbes-Dennis, Ernan and
   Bottome, Phyllis
Fordham, Michael
Forrester, Mrs. Anne and John
Frankfort, Dr. Hans, the late
Fredman, Rafael
Freshfield, J. W.

Gabo, N.
Gardiner, Miss Margaret (12)
Geluwe, Gustave van
Gibberd, Frederick
Gibson, George (U.S.A.)
Gibson, George W. (2) (U.S.A.)
Gibson-Smith, Ian (4)
Gill, Leslie
Gilvarry, James jr. (U.S.A.)
Gimpel Fils Gallery (14)
Giron, Robert
Glasgow Art Gallery

Goodhue, Walter S.
Gordan, A.
Grady, James H. (U.S.A.)
Graaf, Jan de (U.S.A.)
Gray, Mrs. Nicolete (2)
Grand Rapids Gallery (U.S.A.)
Gregory, E. C. (7)
Grigson, Geoffrey
Guggenheim Museum, New York,
   U.S.A.
Guggenheim, Mrs. Peggy
Guthrie, A.

Harris, R. V.
Harrison, Stephen
Harvey, Mrs. Grace and Len
Hatfield College, (2)
Havinden, Ashley
Hélion, Jean (France)
Henderson, Nigel
Hepworth, Miss Barbara (24)
Hepworth, H. R. (2)
Hertfordshire County Council (2)
Hitchcock, Henry Russell
Hodgkin, Mrs. M. C.
Hodgkins, Miss E. M. (3)
Hodin, Mrs. Pamela and Dr. J. P.
Honda, H. (Japan)
Hooper, Mrs. E. J.
Hulton, Mrs. Nita and Edward (4)
Hunter, Miss Caroline (U.S.A.)

International Business Machines
   Corporation, New York, U.S.A.

Jackman, Mrs. N. R. (U.S.A.)
Jackson, Arthur
Jackson, Mrs. Martha K. (2)
Jakovski, Anatole
James, Edward
Jaray, S. (2)
Jones, Miss Bertha
Jowett, P. H.
Jowitt, Lady

Kauffer, E. McKnight, the late
Kaye, Miss (2)
Kaye, S.
Kearley, C.
Keene, Ralph
Kennedy, Wasnett
Kent-Bragaline Inc. (U.S.A.)
Kessler, Mrs.

Laing Art Gallery, Newcastle
Langdon, Basil
Laurence, Major L.
Leeds City Art Gallery
Lefevre Gallery

11

Legge, Miss Rhoda
Le Mare, Bernard
Lescaze, William (U.S.A.)
Levin, Mr. and Mrs. I. (U.S.A.)
Lewis, David (2)
London Airport
Ludington, Wright S. (U.S.A.)
Lye, Len

Mabille, Marcelle
MacCaw, Miss
McColgan, Miss Kathleen
Macdonald, Mrs. L. and the late
 Duncan (4)
Manchester City Art Gallery (3)
Markham, H.
Marsh, Sir Edward, the late
Martin, Mrs. S. and Dr. J. L. (32)
May, R. D. S. (3)
Meredith, Burgess (U. S. A.)
Mewton, Roy
Meynell, Francis
Michigan University, Ann Arbor,
 U. S. A.
Miller Company, Meriden, U.S.A.
Moore, Henry
Moore, Miss Vera (3)
Morland, Mrs. Dorothy
Morris, Mrs. Suzy and G. L. K.
 (U.S.A.)
Morrish, H. J.
Morton, A. J. F. (3)
Mott, E. H.
Moyens, H. Marc (U.S.A.)
Mull, Miss Jane (U.S.A.)
Munson Williams Proctor Institute,
 New York, U.S.A.
Murray, F. L. S. (12)
Murray, R. D., Jr. (U.S.A.)
Murray, W. Staite (2)
Museum of Modern Art, New York,
 U.S.A.
Myers, Mrs. Elsie (2)

Nagata, S. (Japan)
Nagelschmidt, Mrs. Betty (3)
Nalle, Eugene (U.S.A.)
Napper, Jack
Nash, Paul, the late (2)
New South Wales National
 Gallery, Australia
Newberry, John S. (U.S.A.)
Ney, Miss Marie
Neylan, Mrs.
Nicholson, Mrs. E. Q. and the late
 Christopher (5)
Nicholson, Lady
Nicholson, Miss Jenny (2)
Nicholson, Mrs. Winifred (16)

Nicholson, Sir William, the late
Nixon, Mrs. Edna
Noyes, Miss (2)

Ody, R. H. M.
Ogilvie, Mrs. Margaret and
 Lawrence
Ohara Museum, Kurashiki, Japan
Oliver, Alan (2)
Oliver, Mrs. P. (U.S.A.)
Oppenheim, D. L. M.
Ordeig, Jose

Pasmore, Victor
Pearce, Margaret Ricardo
Péchere, Paul (2)
Peters, Donald (U.S.A.)
Philadelphia Museum, Gallatin
 Collection, U.S.A.
Picher, William S. (U.S.A.)
Pilkington, Miss
Powell, Lydia Bond
Pritchard, J. C. (2)

Rachliss, Michael
Raine, Miss Kathleen (2)
Rainier, Miss Priaulx
Ramsden, E. H. (2)
S.S. Rangitane, New Zealand
 Shipping Co. (2)
Ravelli, Baron
Read, Sir Herbert and Lady (4)
Rebay, Baroness von (2)
Reddihough, C. S. (25)
Reid, A. J. McN.
Rio de Janeiro, Museu de Arte
 Moderna, Brazil (2)
Roberts, Lady Cecilia, the late (8)
Roberts, Mrs. Nancy (5)
Roberts, Wilfred (3)
Robertson, J. W. Howard
Robinson, Mrs. Joan
Root, Edward (4) (U.S.A.)
Rosner, D.
Rowntree, Kenneth (3)
Russ, Mrs. M. W. V.

Sachs, Paul J. (U.S.A.)
Sackville-West, Hon. Edward
Sadler, Sir Michael, the late (12)
Seacrest, Frederick (U.S.A.)
Seuphor, Michel (France)
Sewter, A. C.
Shimbum, Mainichi (2) (Japan)
Singer, F.
Slater, Mrs. Moyra
Slater, Humphrey
Smith College Museum,
 Northampton, Mass., U.S.A.

Smith, Roland (U.S.A.)
Stanton, Francis (U.S.A.)
Steel, G. Hammond
Stokes, Adrian (5)
Straight, Michael
Straight, Whitney (4)
Strausz-Hupé, Robert
Stuart-Piggott, Mrs.
Summerson, John (8)
Sutherland, Graham
Sutherland, Miss Helen (36)
Swindon Art Gallery
Sydney Art Gallery, Australia (2)

Tachmindji, M. A.
Tambimuttu, M. J.
Tate Gallery (3)
Thompson, G. David (4) (U.S.A.)
Tibbetts, Miss
"Time and Life", London
Tokyo Art Gallery, Japan (2)
Toledo Art Gallery, U.S.A.
Toronto Art Gallery, Canada (3)
Trent, Lord
Turner, I. P.
Turner, Mrs. M. A. C. and H. J. (3)
Twentyman, T.

Val, Van der (4) (Holland)
Valentin, Curt, the late
Vancouver Art Gallery, Canada
Venice, Galleria d'Arte Moderna,
 Italy
Ventris, Michael
Vibe-Hastrup, Mrs. Aase and
 Ikse (Denmark)

Walden, Lady Howard de
Walker Art Centre, Minneapolis,
 U.S.A. (2)
Walker, J. A. Paton
Wardell, Simon (U.S.A.)
Watson, Peter
Wells, John (5)
White, Miss Pamela
Whiting, Miss Gladys (2)
Whitworth Institute, Manchester
Williams, G. F.
Williams, Joan
Wilson, Colin
Winn, Godfrey
Wishart, Mrs. Lorna
Wittman, M. (Belgium)
Wolfenden, G.
Wood, Christopher, the late (2)
Woodford, F. J. (3)

Zuckerman, Lady Joan and Solly
Zurcher, Victor (U.S.A.)

figures in brackets denote number of works in owner's possession.

INTRODUCTION by Herbert Read

the plastic virtues: purity, unity, and truth, keep nature in subjection—APOLLINAIRE

BEN NICHOLSON is the leading representative in Great Britain of that tendency in art which has been called *abstract*, and it might be best, therefore, to begin this *INTRODUCTION* with some account of the historical origins of this tendency, to the end that we may approach the work of our artist equipped with some understanding of its stylistic significance.

It should be realised in the first place that the tendency to abstraction in art is by no means specifically modern. It has recurred repeatedly throughout the history of art, and was already recognized as an historical phenomenon, and called "abstract", before the modern movement came into being. Wilhelm Worringer's brilliant essay on *Abstraktion und Einfühlung*, for example, was written in 1906 and published in 1908, and in this essay all the features which distinguish abstract art as such are clearly recognized. Indeed, it is possible that the *theory* of abstract art not only preceded the practice of it in modern times, but actually inspired and influenced its development. Worringer's essay was published in Munich, and in the first two years of its publication three editions were issued. In Munich, at this time, lived Wassily Kandinsky, a Russian painter who was to become the most consistent exponent of abstract art in Europe. His first paintings in this style date from 1909–10, and in the latter year he wrote *Über das Geistige in der Kunst* (Concerning the Spiritual in Art) which is the earliest exposition of abstract art from the point of view of a practising painter.[1] The Cubist movement in Paris was taking shape at the same time, though it is doubtful whether anything as intransigently abstract as Kandinsky's "Improvisations" of

1910 was painted before that year (it was in the summer of 1910 that Picasso, in the Catalan village of Cadaqués, "brought Cubism nearer than ever to an art of abstract design").[2] It will be part of my argument that the abstract movement in modern art corresponds to a certain psychological necessity which is widely diffused in the world to-day, and it is therefore idle to speculate on priorities in the formulation of a modern abstract style. But one more significant fact might be mentioned—to Munich in 1909 came Naum Gabo, a medical student from Russia, who was to become one of the founders of the abstract movement known as Constructivism. Gabo met Kandinsky in Munich the following year.

Worringer's famous essay has never been translated into English, but a very adequate summary of it was made by T. E. Hulme in a lecture he delivered in 1914, published later in the collection of his writings entitled *Speculations*.[3] An extensive quotation from this "abstract" would seem to be justified in the present context.

After pointing out that there are two kinds of art, geometrical and vital, absolutely distinct from one another, and that these two arts are not modifications of one and the same art, but pursue different aims

---

[1] an English translation under the title *The Art of Spiritual Harmony* was made by Michael Sadleir and published in London in 1914. A new translation from a revised text under the title, *Concerning the Spiritual in Art*, was published in New York (Wittenborn, Schultz, Inc.) in 1947

[2] Cf. *Picasso: Fifty Years of his Art*, by Alfred H. Barr, Jr., New York (Museum of Modern Art), 1946, p. 73

[3] London (Kegan Paul), 1924, pp. 75–109

13

and are created for the satisfaction of different necessities of the mind, Hulme (closely following Worringer's text) goes on to define the tendencies underlying each type. Vital art, he writes,

"as contrasted with geometrical art can be broadly described as naturalism or realism—using these words in their widest sense and entirely excluding the mere imitation of nature. The source of the pleasure felt by the spectator before the products of art of this kind is a feeling of increased vitality, a process which the German writers on æsthetics call empathy (Einfühlung). This process is perhaps a little too complicated for me to describe it shortly here, but putting the matter in general terms, we can say that any work of art we find beautiful is an

TORCELLO *detail of cathedral mosaic 12th century*

objectification of our own pleasure in activity, and our own vitality. The worth of a line or form consists in the value of the life which it contains for us. Putting the matter more simply we may say that in this art there is always a feeling of liking for, and pleasure in, the forms and movements to be found in nature. It is obvious therefore that this art can only occur in a people whose relation to outside nature is such that it admits of this feeling of pleasure in its contemplation.

"Turn now to geometrical art. It most obviously exhibits no delight in nature and no striving after vitality. Its forms are always what can be described as stiff and lifeless. The dead form of a pyramid and the suppression of life in a Byzantine mosaic show that behind these arts there must have been an impulse the direct opposite of that which finds satisfaction in the naturalism of Greek and Renaissance art.

"This is what Worringer calls the *tendency to abstraction.*

"What is the nature of this tendency? What is the condition of mind of the people whose art is governed by it?

"It can be described most generally as a feeling of separation in the face of outside nature.

"While a naturalistic art is the result of a happy pantheistic relation between man and the outside

PICASSO *la jeune fille á la mandoline 1910*
collection Roland Penrose

14

KANDINSKY   *composition 4 1911*

world, the tendency to abstraction, on the contrary, occurs in races whose attitude to the outside world is the exact contrary of this. This feeling of separation naturally takes different forms at different levels of culture."

These various types of abstract art (and, indeed, various types of naturalistic art) can be illustrated from different historical periods. There is the abstraction of peoples who live in a world whose lack of order and seeming arbitrariness must inspire them with a certain fear (the art of the Neolithic period, or of primitive races whose low technological abilities leave them at the mercy of drought, famine, and other "visitations"—the Australian aborigines, for example). There is also the abstraction of highly-developed civilizations such as the Egyptian, Indian, and Byzantine, where the feeling of human separateness has a metaphysical or religious basis. Hulme contrasts the primitive and Byzantine attitudes. "There is a certain likeness and a certain unlikeness in relation to man and the outside world. The primitive springs from what we have called a kind of mental space-shyness, which is really an attitude of fear before the world; the Byzantine from what may be called, inaccurately, a kind of contempt for the world. Though these two attitudes differ very much, yet there is a common element in the idea of separation as opposed to the more intimate feeling towards

the world in classical and renaissance thought."

Worringer, who to some extent based himself on earlier philosophers of art like Lipps and Riegl, elaborated his theory, as I have already pointed out, before the "tendency to abstraction" made its appearance in modern art, and it may well be asked how and why such a tendency should have made its appearance in our own time, and whether the same theoretical hypothesis will serve for both the historical types of abstract art in the past and those of the present day. I have already suggested that Worringer's theories may have been a direct inspiration of the modern tendency, but I doubt if what may have begun in this artificial way would have assumed the proportions of a world-wide movement affecting all the arts (for the music of a composer like

PICASSO   *tête (collage) 1914*
collection Roland Penrose

15

Schonberg comes into comparison, as well as the main trend of modern architecture) unless there had been some underlying and urgent need for this type of expression. As a matter of fact, philosophy had for many years been preparing the ground for such a development, and to Worringer's "Raumscheu" or space-shyness corresponds Heidegger's "Angst" or dread, which is merely space-shyness (fear of "nothingness") in cosmic dimensions. In this connection I find it highly significant that it has been men of the metaphysically anguished races (Russian, German, Dutch) who have developed abstract art to its logical extremes, while artists who belong to the races who in the past were exponents of the naturalistic tradition (Picasso, Chirico, Severini) have consistently shied away from pure abstraction. Picasso, in particular, has more than once violently affirmed the naturalistic basis of his art.

Existentialism is by no means a universal philosophy,

JUAN GRIS   *violin and glass 1918*
collection Andre Lefevre

and we cannot assume that an abstract art giving perfect expression to this metaphysical attitude will ever be generally accepted in any country (though a decay of modern civilization involving such a universal pessimism is not inconceivable). At present the adoption of such an attitude, whether in philosophy or art, is a matter for individual choice. But here we come upon a final complexity, not foreseen by Worringer or Hulme. They did, indeed, acknowledge the co-existence, in past epochs, of abstract and naturalistic styles, and Worringer's *Egyptian Art*,[1] for example, is a consideration of some of the problems suggested by this phenomenon. But the social and psychological conditions are treated as collective expressions arising from a particular group or class. What we must now affirm is the possibility, not merely of an individual reaction, but even of the alternation, within the individual consciousness, of both attitudes. In a superficial sense, this may be interpreted as no more than an alternation of optimistic and pessimistic moods. Admitting the existentialist analysis of man's position in the universe, it is still possible for the individual to react positively or negatively, with despair or with courage, with fear or with confidence. In certain cases it seems possible for an individual to alternate between the extremes represented by this polarity —to tend in one psychological phase towards an affirmation of the world which results in a naturalistic style, and in another psychological phase to tend towards a rejection of that world which results in an abstract style of art. Ben Nicholson is an artist of this complex type.

II

To describe Ben Nicholson as a "complex" artist immediately introduces a paradox, for in another sense no artist could be more free from the introspective self-consciousness implied by such a

---

[1] translated by Bernard Rackham. London (Putnam) 1928

16

word. He is in no sense an intellectual or meta-physical painter. All his development has proceeded from the play of a native sensibility with the materials of his craft. No painter could be less ideological, in the sense of using his craft to illustrate a thesis. Art for him has been a continuous process of exploration and discovery, and each conquest of a new territory has served as the base for a new expedition. He will often call these discoveries "ideas", but an idea is something "to work on", a concrete material of sensation to mould or manipulate sensuously. Certain symbols remain constant: the jug in the early naive painting of 1911 (*plate* 1) reappears repeatedly, and is present in the latest works of 1947–8. Colour, too, is a constant factor—the candid, gay colours of fruits, playing cards, fishing floats, and glazed pottery. Chiaroscuro is eliminated, or reduced to precise limits, as in a Byzantine mosaic. But with these constant factors the artist creates infinite variations, and it is in the exploitation of these variations that he quite naturally, without conscious deliberation, arrives at the extremes of realism and abstraction. The contemporaneous contrasts presented in such pairs as *plates* 123–4, 127–8, 162 and 164 represent, not a contradiction, not a dichotomy of any kind, but the same sensibility with a different visual "reson-ance". The distinction is not one that can be usefully related to the historical categories of "analytical" and "synthetic" cubism. The abstractions, in any such comparison, are in no sense derived from a given subject, nor is a subject imposed on a pre-determined architectural structure (in the manner of Juan Gris). The formal relations may emerge from the objective world, as the summary representations of walls, windows and doors in the painting of Halse Town (*plate* 109); and something very near, in a formal geometric sense, may be repeated in an abstrac-tion like that which is illustrated on the same page (*plate* 110). But the similarities are merely due to the limitations of geometrical formulas, from which the

artist rarely frees himself (*plates* 25 and 26 represent the limits of such freedom, and are for that reason exceptional). In general one might say that our artist always moors his sensibility to a geometrical pier—he is never merely an impressionist, content to record some hazy and fleeting aspect of the visible world. He always seeks the utmost clarity and precision, but succeeds in combining these qualities with the complexity demanded by the polar tension (realism : abstraction) already mentioned.

The simplicity and fewness of the formal symbols employed by this artist do not constitute a limitation on his powers of invention—on the contrary, he revels in the multiplicity of the variations he can command with these limited means, for like all great artists he realises that beauty is a product of self-imposed difficulties. In this respect his work may be compared with certain types of ornament—Celtic,

MONDRIAN *c.* 1937   *private collection*

Romanesque and Moslem—where the same richness emerges from a similar limitation. Some words of Henri Focillon's may be quoted in this connection:

"The most rigorous rules, apparently intended to impoverish and standardize formal material, are precisely those which, with an almost fantastic wealth of variations and of metamorphoses, best illuminate its superb vitality. What could be more removed from life, from its ease and its flexibility, than the geometric combinations of Moslem ornament? These combinations are produced by mathematical reasoning. They are based upon cold calculation; they are reducible to patterns of the utmost aridity. But deep within them a sort of fever seems to goad on and multiply the shapes; some mysterious genius of complication interlocks, enfolds, disorganizes, and reorganizes the entire labyrinth. Their very immobility sparkles with metamorphoses. Whether they be read as voids or as solids, as vertical axes or as diagonals, each one of them both withholds the secret and exposes the reality of an immense number of possibilities. An analogous phenomenon occurs in Romanesque sculpture. Here abstract form is both stem and support for a strange, chimerical image of animal and human life; here monsters that are shackled permanently to an architectural and ornamental definition are yet endlessly reborn in so many different ways that their captivity mocks both us and itself. Form becomes a *rinceau*, a double-headed eagle, a mermaid, a duel of warriors. It duplicates, coils back upon, and devours its own shape. Without once trespassing its limits or falsifying its principles, this protean monster rouses up, and unrolls its demented existence—an existence that is merely the turmoil and the undulation of a single, simple form."[1]

This paragraph, I believe, beautifully describes the "internal logic" of the art of Ben Nicholson, but it may be thought that it lays it open to the charge of *mere decorativeness*, a charge which does not gain in intelligence by being repeated by critics who ought to know better. Apart from the truth of Ruskin's

CYPRUS,
EARLY
BRONZE AGE

*terracotta
figure of
The Goddess of Fecundity*

1 *The Life of Forms in Art.* translated by Charles Beecher Hogan and George Kubler. 2nd edn. New York (Wittenborn, Schultz, Inc.), 1948, p. 6

assertion, that all art is decorative in the degree that it is art, it is demonstrable that Ben Nicholson's painting is not even decorative in the sense implied by the derogatory use of the word. In this sense "decorative" is descriptive of two-dimensional patterns without any fundamental content. But form, as Focillon remarks, is never "the catch-as-catch-can garment of subject matter" (the mistake made by Juan Gris); "form has a meaning—but it is a meaning entirely its own, a personal and specific value that must not be confused with the attributes we impose upon it". In this sense, the formal values of Ben Nicholson's paintings have the same values as the forms of Poussin or Rembrandt or Cézanne. They are constructions in space and matter, with all the attributes which such constructions can possess—rhythm, balance, chiaroscuro, and concrete finality. What such critics presumably mean is that such works of art are devoid of mythical content, of poetic "story". One must admit that this is true, but at the same time ask whether the critic is prepared to exclude from the highest categories of art a painting of bamboo shoots by Wu Chen or of apples by Cézanne, equally devoid of mythological content. It is not possible to accept certain still-life compositions of Ben Nicholson's (*plates* 16, 21) and at the same time reject his severe abstractions (*plates* 117, 118) without confessing to a prejudice which has nothing to do with the essential qualities of art. From this point of view the reader might study the two compositions which are confronted in *plates* 123 and 124. Nicholson himself, in the *Notes on Abstract Art* which are reprinted in this volume, speaks of the "poetic idea" as distinct from the "literary content" of a painting. In the same sense one might say that one should never confuse the poetry and the iconography of a painting. There is no art without poetry, but iconography is irrelevant, except as a promoter of poetry.

EARLY BRITISH
courtesy of British Museum

bronze with sunk enamel

III

Sensibility is a physical endowment, inherited rather than acquired, and in this respect Ben Nicholson was born with a silver spoon in his mouth. His father, Sir William Nicholson, was one of the most distinguished representatives in our country of Whistlerian subtleties, of a tradition at once sensitive and intelligent, if a little lacking in poetic invention. But on the maternal side there are affinities no less significant, for the romantic rhetoric of his uncle, James Pryde, though never a direct influence, indicates perhaps the source of a dynamic energy which has driven the scion of such a formidable stock to new growths. Apart from these hereditary factors, the favours of fortune were prolonged in an early environment of accepted æsthetic standards, of activities and conversations which all tended to preserve and educate the natal endowments. Academic education was perfunctory; the real education was an apprenticeship in artists' studios, in travel, in visual experience. There was a fruitful friendship with Christopher Wood, an artist equally endowed with sensibility, sympathetic in outlook and aims. Together they worked out certain simplifications of landscape, experimented in colour, made contact with some remnants of folk art in remote fishing villages. But equally significant was the impact of the School of Paris—the still-lifes of Picasso and Braque, the collages of Juan Gris, the formal simplifications of Jean

Arp and the fantasy of Joan Miró. Distinct, and not less important, was an understanding of the sculptural vision of Barbara Hepworth, and finally and most decisively, the revelation of plastic purity communicated by Piet Mondrian. Mondrian's "neo-plasticism" was a search for what he called "a clear vision of true reality", an impersonal art "unconditioned by subjective feeling and conception". There are many works of Ben Nicholson which conform to the strict canons of neo-plasticism (*plates* 72–6, 81, 89–92, 96–100, 105–7, 123, 129–130, 147–9, 199, etc.) and they now spread over a period of at least fifteen years, and continue to be produced. But, as I have already explained, they represent only one particular resonance of the artist's sensibility. Mondrian had a vivid "life of forms" within his impersonal, non-figurative, anti-naturalistic convention; but he remained fixed at one extreme of the existential axis. Ben Nicholson has never accepted such an extreme position, but has expressed the whole diapason of æsthetic vibrations encountered by an open sensibility in its experience of reality. Mondrian's search for a "true" reality was a search for the absolute; but

BARBARA HEPWORTH
collection T. A. Tachmindji

involute white stone 1946
size 10½″

the artist lives and has his being in immediacy, in intuition, in a certain "animal faith". Art is a subjective process of individuation, and its products are metamorphic, illogical. Art is variety; art is adventure.

It would be presumptuous to express any judgment on the work of a painter who is still intensely active, but, as this volume sufficiently shows, his achievement is already considerable, and the consistency of that achievement, its unfailing revelation of a faultless sensibility and its fountain-like projection of varied forms from a seemingly inexhaustible source, require us to recognize in Ben Nicholson one of the major artists of our time. It is not necessary to claim for him virtues which belong to natures essentially different—there are qualities, like monumentality and humanism, which his genius does not encompass. That his art serves as a prototype for monumentality, as an illustration of architectonic virtues, is evident from the interest it has always held for contemporary architects; and humanism is a prejudice which the modern artist can afford to ignore, as it was ignored before the Renaissance. As for the social relevance of such art as Ben Nicholson's, it has the overwhelming relevance of any extension of the visual faculty. "It is the social function of great poets and artists continually to renew the appearance nature has for the eyes of men. Without poets, without artists, men would soon weary of nature's monotony", wrote Apollinaire. It is impossible to underestimate the biological significance of that intensity of perception, that renewal of the sensibility, which springs from the creation and appreciation of original works of art. In this sense the work of Ben Nicholson is peculiarly significant in that with relatively simple and direct means it produces the intensest vibrations of the æsthetic sensibility.

20

BIBLIOGRAPHY

Helen Sutherland: *Foreword to exhibition at Beaux Arts Gallery, 1926.*

H. S. Ede: *"Ben Nicholson, Winifred Nicholson, and William Staite Murray"*, ARTWORK, No. 16, pp. 262–8, 1928.

Charles Marriott: *"Ben Nicholson"*, THE TIMES, March 7, 1930.

C. S. Reddihough: *Foreword to exhibition at Lefevre Gallery, March 1930.*

Paul Nash: *"A Painter and a Sculptor"*, WEEK-END REVIEW, p. 613, November 19, 1932.

H. S. Ede: *Foreword to exhibition at Tooth & Sons Gallery, 1932.*

Ben Nicholson: *"Aim of the Modern Artist"*, THE STUDIO, p. 333, December, 1932.

Adrian Stokes: *"Ben Nicholson's Painting"*, THE SPECTATOR, p. 517, October 27, 1933.

Geoffrey Grigson: *"Henry Moore & Ben Nicholson"*, THE BOOKMAN, p. 106, November, 1933.

Ben Nicholson: UNIT ONE, pp. 88–94, Cassell, London, 1934.

Herbert Read: *"Ben Nicholson's Recent Works"*, AXIS, pp. 14–16, No. 2, 1935.

Jan Tschichold: *"On Ben Nicholson's Reliefs"*, AXIS, pp. 16–18, No. 2, 1935.

Anatole Jakovski: *"Ben Nicholson"*, GACETA DE ARTE, Teneriffe, No. 36, October, 1935.

Hugh Gordon Porteous: *"Ben Nicholson"*, NEW ENGLISH WEEKLY, October 3, 1935.

Herbert Read: *"Ben Nicholson and the Future of Painting"*, THE LISTENER, pp. 604–5, October 9, 1935.

Paul Nash: *"Ben Nicholson's Carved Reliefs"*, THE ARCHITECTURAL REVIEW, pp. 142–3, October, 1935.

Hugh Gordon Porteous: *"Ben Nicholson"*, THE SCOTTISH BOOK-MAN, pp. 70–2, December, 1935.

Geoffrey Grigson: *"Ben Nicholson"*, THE ARTS TO-DAY, pp. 104–5, Bodley Head, London, 1935.

Alfred H. Barr, Jun.: CUBISM AND ABSTRACT ART, pp. 200–1, Museum of Modern Art, New York, 1936.

Adrian Stokes: *"Ben Nicholson at the Lefevre Galleries"*, THE SPECTATOR, March 19, 1937.

Ben Nicholson: *"Quotations"*, CIRCLE, p. 75, Faber & Faber, London, 1937.

Co-editor with J. L. Martin and N. Gabo of CIRCLE, *International Survey of Constructive Art*, Faber & Faber, London, 1937.

Herbert Read: *"L'Art Contemporain en Angleterre"*, CAHIERS D'ART, Nos. 1–2, pp. 32, 37, 40, Paris, 1938.

John Summerson: *"Abstract Artists"*, THE LISTENER, pp. 574–5, March 16, 1939.

Herbert Read: *"The Development of Ben Nicholson"*, LONDON BULLETIN, No. 11, p. 9.

J. L. Martin: *"Architecture and the Painter, with special reference to the work of Ben Nicholson"*, FOCUS, No. 3, pp. 60–7, 1939.

Herbert Read: *"Trois Sculpteurs Anglais"*, XX SIECLE, No. 1, pp. 44–5, Paris, 1939.

G. L. K. Morris: *Museum of Living Art*, New York, Critical Note 98, Catalogue, 1940.

Ben Nicholson: *"Notes on Abstract Art"*, HORIZON, pp. 272–6, October, 1941.

Ben Nicholson: *"Notes on Abstract Art"*, ART OF THIS CENTURY, New York, pp. 93, 143–6, 1942.

E. H. Ramsden: *"Contrasts and Comparisons between Old Masters and New"*, WORLD REVIEW, pp. 47, 55, December, 1943.

Herbert Read: *"A Coat of Many Colours"*, BEN NICHOLSON, pp. 79–87, Routledge, London, 1945.

Michael Ayrton: *"Ben Nicholson"*, THE SPECTATOR, October 12, 1945.

Patrick Heron: *"Ben Nicholson"*, NEW ENGLISH WEEKLY, October 18, 1945.

E. H. Ramsden: *"Ben Nicholson, Constructivist"*, THE STUDIO, pp. 179–81, December, 1945.

Humphrey Slater: *"A Note on the Importance of Ben Nicholson"*, POLEMIC, No. 2, pp. 49–51, 1946.

Michael Rothenstein: *"Looking at Paintings"*, BEN NICHOLSON, pp. 46, 47, 60, Routledge, London, 1947.

Robin Ironside: *"British Painting Since 1939"*, pp. 18, 22–3, The British Council, 1947.

Herbert Read: *"Tendances récentes dans l'art anglais"*, LES ARTS PLASTIQUES, Nos. 1–2, pp. 35–7, Brussels, 1948.

J. P. Hodin: *"Ben Nicholson"*, PALETTEN, No. 1, pp. 28–30, Gothenberg, 1948.

Henry-Russell Hitchcock: *"Painting Toward Architecture"*, pp. 90–1, Miller Company Collection of Abstract Art, Duell, Sloane & Pearce, New York, 1948.

John Russell: *"From Sickert to 1948"*, pp. 103–4, Lund Humphries, London, 1948.

John Summerson: *"Ben Nicholson"*, PENGUIN MODERN PAINTERS July, 1948.

Eduardo Westerdahl: *"Ben Nicholson"*, CABALGATA, Buenos Aires, August, 1948.

Charles Estienne: *"Peinture et Culture Anglaises"*, Catalogue of exhibition *"Jeune Peinture en Grande-Bretagne"*, Galerie René Drouin, Paris, 1948.

James Thrall Soby: *"Contemporary Painters"*, BEN NICHOLSON, pp. 130–3, Museum of Modern Art, New York, 1949.

The Times Literary Supplement, January 22, p. 54, London, 1949.

Nicolete Gray: *"Ben Nicholson"*, THE ARCHITECTURAL REVIEW, pp. 210, 244, May, 1949.

John Summerson: *"Ben Nicholson"*, BURLINGTON MAGAZINE, p. 237, August, 1949.

Ivo Jarosy: *"Der Maler Ben Nicholson"*, BLICK, pp. 34, 35, Hamburg, July, 1949.

J. P. Hodin: *"Ben Nicholson"*, THE CORNISH REVIEW, pp. 83–8, Autumn, 1949.

J. L. Martin: *"The World Inside a Frame"*, THE LISTENER, p. 148, January 27, 1949.

Margot Eates: *"Ben Nicholson"*, EIDOS, No. 1, London, June, 1950.

Eduardo Westerdahl: *"Ben Nicholson y su arte"*, INSULA, Madrid, May 15, 1950.

Eduardo Westerdahl: *"Espiritu e Clima de Ben Nicholson"*, CLIMA, Numero 1, Anno 1, Monte Video, Uruguay, 1950.

Anthony Bertram: *"A Century of British Painting 1851–1951"*, pp. 10, 90, 98, 99, 103, 113, THE STUDIO, 1951.

David Lewis: *"Ben Nicholson, another view"*, THE STUDIO, pp. 184–7, London, May, 1952.

Patrick Heron: *"Ben Nicholson"*, THE NEW STATESMAN, p. 584, May 17, 1952.

John Berger: *"Poetic Accuracy"*, ART NEWS AND REVIEW, Vol. 4, No. 8, p. 4, 1952.

Henry-Russell Hitchcock: *Introduction to Catalogue Durlacher Bros.*, New York, November, 1952.

Lawrence Alloway: "*Non-figurative art in England*", ARTE VISIVI, p. 13, Nos. 6–7, Rome, 1952.

Gordon Bailey Washburn: "*The 1952 International*", CARNEGIE MAGAZINE, p. 299, Pittsburgh, November, 1952.

A. C. Sewter: "*Painting and Architecture in Renaissance and Modern Times*", pp. 13, 15, 16, Tiranti Ltd., London, 1952.

Herbert Read: "*The Philosophy of Modern Art*", pp. 216–25, Faber, London, 1952.

Adrian Heath: "*Ben Nicholson*", ABSTRACT PAINTING, pp. 17, 18, Tiranti, 1953.

Herta Wescher: "*Ben Nicholson*", L'ART D'AUJOURD'HUI, pp. 10, 11, Paris, March, 1953.

Frank McEwen: "*Nouvelle Ecole Anglaise*", LE SOLEIL NOIRE, p. 160, Nos. 3 & 4, Paris, 1953.

Eric Newton: "*Ben Nicholson*", BRITAIN TODAY, p. 28, June, 1954.

J. P. Hodin: "*Ben Nicholson*", ART NEWS AND REVIEW, p. 1, No. 13, Vol. VI, July 24, 1954.

Herbert Read: "*Le due tendenze Inglesi*", LA BIENNALE DI VENEZIA pp. 53–6, Nos. 19–20, Venice, October, 1954.

J. P. Hodin: "*Ben Nicholson, il pitagoreo*", LA BIENNALE DI VENEZIA, pp. 59–61, Nos. 19–20, Venice, October, 1954.

Leon Dégand: "*La Biennale de Venise*" ART D'AUJOURD'HUI, p. 24, Paris, September, 1954.

J. P. Hodin: "*Ben Nicholson*", KRONIK VAN KUNST EN KULTUUR, pp. 126–31, No. 7, Amsterdam, 1954.

J. P. Hodin: "*Ben Nicholson*" ART NEWS AND REVIEW, No. 13, London, 1954.

Frank McEwen: "*Ben Nicholson*", DICTIONNAIRE DE LA PEINTURE MODERNE, Ed. Fernan Hazan, Paris, 1954.

Emily Genauer: "*Venice Biennale*", NEW YORK HERALD TRIBUNE, August 15 and August 22, 1954.

Herbert Read: Introduction to catalogue of exhibition in British Pavilion, XXVIII Biennale, Venice, 1954.

Herbert Read: Introduction to catalogue of exhibition at the Stedilijk Museum, Amsterdam, November, 1954.

David Lewis: "*Ben Nicholson*", SELE ARTE, pp. 34, 35, 50, No. 12, Milan, August, 1954.

Gillo Dorfles: "*Ben Nicholson*", AUT-AUT, p. 337, No. 22, Milan, 1954.

Rudolph Arnheim: "*Art and Visual Perception*", pp. 39, 40, 106, pub. University of California Press, U.S.A., 1954.

David Lewis: "*Ben Nicholson*", AUJOURD'HUI, ART ET ARCHITECTURE, No. 1, Paris, January, 1955.

Alain Jouffroy: "*Ben Nicholson au Musée d'Art Moderne*", ARTS, Paris, January 25, 1955.

"*Regards sur Ben Nicholson*", pub. The British Council, Paris, 1955.

Robert Geerts: "*Ben Nicholson, un maître de l'art abstrait*", LA DERNIERE HEURE, Brussels, March 8, 1955.

R. V. Gindertael: "*Ben Nicholson au Musée Nationale d'Art Moderne (Paris)*", LES BEAUX ARTS, pp. 12, 13, Brussels, January 28, 1955.

Charles Bernard: "*Ben Nicholson au Palais des Beaux Arts*", LA NATION BELGE, Brussels, May 3, 1955.

E. Storck: "*Ben Nicholson*", LA LIBRE BELGE, Brussels, May 5, 1955.

Leon-Louis Soisset: "*Le peintre anglais Ben Nicholson*", LA NOUVELLE GAZETTE, Brussels, May 8, 1955.

Herta Wescher: "*Ben Nicholson; Musée d'Art Moderne*", CIMAISE, No. 5, Paris, 1955.

J. P. Hodin: "*Ben Nicholson, peintre de l'équilibre et de l'harmonie*", LES BEAUX-ARTS, pp. 1, 3, Brussels, March 4, 1955.

Herbert Read: Introduction to catalogue of exhibition at the Musée Nationale d'Art Moderne, Paris, January, 1955.

Herbert Read: Introduction to catalogue of exhibition at the Palais Royale des Beaux Arts, Brussels, March, 1955.

Herbert Read: Introduction to catalogue of exhibition at the Kunsthalle, Zürich, April, 1955.

J. P. Hodin: "*Ben Nicholson*", DOMUS, Milan, No. 305, 1955.

Michel Seuphor: "*Fernand Léger and Ben Nicholson*", ARTS-DIGEST, New York, April 1, 1955.

J. P. Hodin: "*Ben Nicholson*", DIE KUNST, pp. 249–52, Munich, April, 1955.

Herbert Read: Revised introduction to catalogue of exhibition at the Tate Gallery, London, June, 1955.

Ben Nicholson: "*Notes*", catalogue of exhibition at the Tate Gallery, London, June, 1955.

BIOGRAPHICAL NOTE

BEN NICHOLSON was born on April 10, 1894 at Denham, Buckinghamshire, the eldest son of the English painter William Nicholson and his Scotch wife, Mabel Pryde, also a painter and sister of James Pryde. He was educated at Heddon Court, Hampstead, and for one term at Gresham School, Holt. Later he attended the Slade School of Art, London, for one term and then studied French at Tours (1911–12), Italian at Milan (1912–13), afterwards spending some months at Madeira (1913–14), and Pasadena, California (1917–18), for reasons of health. He lived in London and North Wales (1914–17) and married the painter Winifred (Dacre) Nicholson, living at Castagnola, Switzerland and in London and Cumberland (1920–31); later he married the sculptor Barbara Hepworth and has since lived in London and Cornwall. By his first wife he had a daughter and two sons, and by his second wife a son and two daughters.

The first one-man exhibition of his work was held at the *Adelphi Gallery* 1922, and later exhibitions at *Paterson Gallery* (with Winifred Nicholson) 1923, *Beaux Arts Gallery* (with Christopher Wood and W. Staite Murray) 1926, *Lefevre Gallery* 1930, *Galérie Georges Bernheim & Cie.*, Paris (with Christopher Wood) 1930, *Bloomsbury Gallery* 1931, *A. Tooth & Sons Gallery* (with Barbara Hepworth) 1932, *Lefevre Gallery* (with Barbara Hepworth) 1933, and at the *Lefevre Gallery* in 1933, 1935, 1937, 1939, 1945, 1947, 1948, 1950, 1952, 1954. A retrospective exhibition of his work was arranged by Sir Philip Hendy at the *Leeds City Art Gallery, Temple Newsam*, in 1944. Exhibition at *Gimpel Fils Gallery*, London, June, 1955.

He was a member of the "7 & 5" (1925–36), "*Unit One*" (1933), and "*Abstraction-Création*", Paris (1933–35), and was, with J. L. Martin and N. Gabo, a co-editor of "*Circle*", International review of Constructive art; Faber & Faber, London, 1937. His "*Notes on Abstract Art*" were published in "*Horizon*" in 1941.

His work was first exhibited in Paris in 1933, at Venice Biennale in 1934, Brussels in 1935, Amsterdam and New York in 1936, and Tokyo in 1952. He has held one-man exhibitions in New York in 1949, 1951, 1952, and 1955, and at the *Phillips Gallery* in Washington in 1951. His work was awarded first prize at the Carnegie International Exhibition at Pittsburgh in 1952 and represented Great Britain at the Venice Biennale in 1954 where it was awarded the "*Ulissi*" prize by the International Jury. He held one-man shows at the *Stedilijk Museum*, Amsterdam in 1954; and at the *Musée d'Art Moderne*, Paris; *Palais des Beaux Arts*, Brussels; *Künsthalle*, Zurich; and *Tate Gallery*, London in 1955. His work is represented in the following public collections: *Tate Gallery; Aberdeen Art Gallery; Arts Council of Great Britain; Birmingham, City Art Gallery; Bristol, City Art Gallery; British Council; Glasgow Art Gallery; Leeds City Art Gallery; Manchester City Art Gallery; Manchester, Whitworth Art Gallery; Newcastle, Laing Art Gallery.*

Ann Arbor, University of Michigan; Buffalo, New York, Albright Gallery; Detroit Institute of Arts; Michigan, Grand Rapids Art Gallery; New York, Guggenheim Museum; New York, Museum of Modern Art; Northampton, Mass., Smith College Museum; Philadelphia Museum; Utica, New York, Munson Williams Procto Institute; Walker Art Centre, Minneapolis; Washington, Phillips Gallery.

Ottawa, National Gallery of Canada; Toronto Art Gallery; Vancouver Art Gallery. Brussels, Palais des Beaux-Arts; Kurashiki, Japan, Ohara Museum; Rio de Janeiro, Museu de Arte Moderna; Sydney, National Gallery of New South Wales; Melbourne, National Gallery; Venice, Galleria Internazionale d'Arte Moderna; Brussels, Musées Royaux des Beaux Arts; and Antwerp, Musée Royale des Beaux Arts.

NOTES ON "ABSTRACT" ART
by Ben Nicholson

ABOUT "abstract" art: I have not yet seen it pointed out that this liberation of form and colour is closely linked with all the other liberations one hears about. I think it ought, perhaps, to come into one of our lists of war-aims. After all, every movement of human life is affected by form and colour, everything we see, touch, think and feel is linked up with it, so that when an artist can use these elements freely and creatively it can be a tremendously potent influence in our lives. The power, for instance, to create space (not "literary" space but actual space) is surely invaluable. I think, too, that so far from "abstract" art being the withdrawal of the artist from reality (into an "ivory tower") it has brought art once again into common every-day life—there is evidence of this in its common spirit with and influence on many things like contemporary architecture, aeroplanes, cars, refrigerators, typography, publicity, electric torches, lipstick holders, etc. But like all the more profound religious, poetic, scientific, musical or artistic ideas its deepest meaning is only understood by a few and the process seems to

BEN NICHOLSON
collection Adrian Stokes

still life 1932-35

colour is an important event, and when critics announce or foretell the death of abstract art they show the same misunderstanding of the freedom of form and colour as the dictators do of the freedom of the individual: putting an end to the liberty of either is, however, a hopeless job, right from the start, as there is only one way of doing so—by putting an end not only to the human race but to every other form of life.

Many people expect one kind of art to exclude all others, but I don't see why all the different forms can't proceed at the same time: there is a place for abstract art, for surrealist art or indeed for an art based more directly on representation, though since abstract art is painting and sculptural expression free and undiluted it must have a special potency of its own.

be that these interpret it to a few more who pass it on to the rest of the world who unconsciously incorporate it in their lives. A Raphael is not a painting in the National Gallery—it is an active force in our lives.

It was interesting that during an exhibition of abstract work which I held in London several people in different professions wrote saying that they felt a common bond between their job and mine: a yacht designer, for instance, wrote that it was a hair's breadth in design which decided the pace or lack of pace in a yacht and that it seemed to be this same hair's breadth in design which decided the power or lack of power in a relief. These people were getting at the roots of the matter far more than those critics who were concerned as to whether they were works of art and if so why (at first sight) they were so unlike the work of Tintoretto. One can say that the problems dealt with in "abstract" art are related to the interplay of forces and, therefore, that any solution reached has a bearing on all interplay between forces: it is related to Arsenal *v.* Tottenham Hotspur quite as much as to the stars in their courses. I think the recent liberation of the powerful forces of form and

BEN NICHOLSON
collection Durlacher Brothers, New York

still life 1948

24

A great deal of painting and sculpture to-day is concerned with the imitation of life, with the imitation of a man, a tree or a flower instead of using colour and form to create its *equivalent*; no one will ask what a tree is supposed to represent and yet, with the most innocent expression in the world, they will ask what a painting or a sculpture or a construction in space is supposed to represent. This equivalent must be conceived within the terms of the medium, it must be pure painting and sculptural expression, since the introduction of anything extraneous means that the conception is adulterated and therefore that it can no longer have a complete application to other forms of life.

One of the main differences between a representational and an abstract painting is that the former can transport you to Greece by a representation of blue skies and seas, olive trees and marble columns, but in order that you may take part in this you will have to concentrate on the painting, whereas the abstract version by its free use of form and colour will be able to give you the actual quality of Greece itself, and this will become a part of the light and space and life in the room—there is no need to concentrate, *it becomes a part of living*.

In painting a "still-life" one takes the simple every-day forms of a bottle—mug—jug—plate-on-table as the basis for the expression of an idea: the forms are not entirely free though they are free to the extent that each object can be seen from as many viewpoints as you wish at one and the same time but the colours are free: bottle-colour for plate, plate-colour for table, or just as you wish and working in this way you have in time not a still-life of objects but an equivalent of something much more like deer passing through a winter forest, over foothills and mountains, through sunlight and shadows in Arizona, Cornwall or Provence and so, inevitably, you eventually at some point discard altogether the forms of even the simplest objects as a basis

BEN NICHOLSON   *still life 1927*
collection H. S. Ede

and work out your idea, not only in free colour but also in free form. To most people this development may sound easy but, for example, although I made my first "abstract" painting in 1923 it wasn't till 1933 that I was able to establish this development. At first the circles were freely drawn and the structure loose with accidental textures, later I valued more the direct contact that could be obtained by flat planes of colour made and controlled

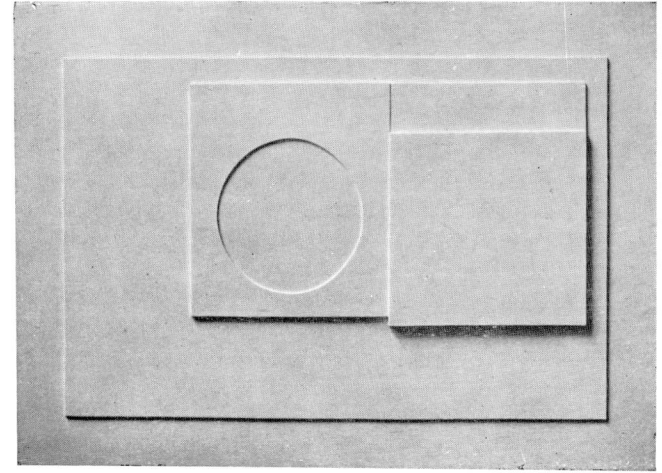

BEN NICHOLSON   *white relief 1935*
collection The British Council

Venus 1946

to an exact pitch and the greater tension obtainable by the use of true circles and rectangles—the superficial appeal became less, but the impact of the idea more direct and therefore more powerful. The geometrical forms often used by abstract artists do not indicate, as has been thought, a conscious and intellectual mathematical approach—a square or a circle in art are nothing in themselves and are alive only in the instinctive and inspirational use an artist can make of them in expressing a poetic idea. If you take a large ultramarine blue and a small cadmium red square and place them on a cool white surface along with a pencilled circle, you can create a most exciting tension between these forces, and if at any time this tension becomes too exciting you can easily, by the smallest mark made by a compass in its centre, transfix the circle like any butterfly!

In a recent number of *Horizon* Grahame Greene, in an article on Read, mentions "a decoration of wires with little balls attached dangling from the ceiling" and suggests, I think, that this is some strange kind of new fashion with no bearing on art. The first time I encountered a Calder (such as this) was in Paris some years ago when I borrowed one and hung it from the centre of the ceiling of a white room overlooking the Seine, and at night, with the river glistening outside, this mobile object turned slowly in the breeze in the light of an electric bulb hung near

its centre—a large black, five small white and one small scarlet ball on their wires turned slowly in and out, around, above, and below each other with their shadows chasing round the white walls in an exciting interchanging movement, suddenly hastening as they turned the corners and disappearing as they crossed the window into the night—it was alive like the hum of the city, like the passing river and the smell of Paris in early spring, but it was not a work of art as so many people think of a work of art—imprisoned in a gold frame or stone-dead on a pedestal in one of our marble-pillar'd mausoleums. But it was "alive" and that, after all, is not a bad qualification for a work of art.

About space-construction: I can explain one aspect of this by an early painting I made of a shop-window in Dieppe (*see plate 58*) though, at the time, this was not made with any conscious idea of space but merely using the shop-window as a theme on which to base an imaginative idea. The name of the shop was "Au Chat Botté", and this set going a train of thought connected with the fairy tales of my childhood and, being in French, and my French being a little mysterious, the words themselves had also an abstract quality—but what was important was that this name was printed in very lovely red lettering on the glass

BEN NICHOLSON   *still life March 21-48*

26

window—*giving one plane*—and in this window were reflections of what was behind me as I looked in—*giving a second plane*—while through the window objects on a table were performing a kind of ballet and forming the "eye" or life-point of the painting—*giving a third plane*. These three planes and all their subsidiary planes were interchangeable so that you could not tell which was real and which unreal, what was reflected and what unreflected, and this created, as I see now, some kind of space or an imaginative world in which one could live.

The same process takes place in making an abstract painting or relief, where, for instance, as the simplest example—you can take a rectangular surface and cut a section of it one plane lower and then in the higher plane cut a circle deeper than, but without touching, the lower plane. *One is immediately conscious that this circle has pierced the lower plane without having touched it*—even a dog or a cat will realize this instantly—and this creates space. The awareness of this is felt subconsciously and it is useless to approach it intellectually as this, so far from helping, only acts as a

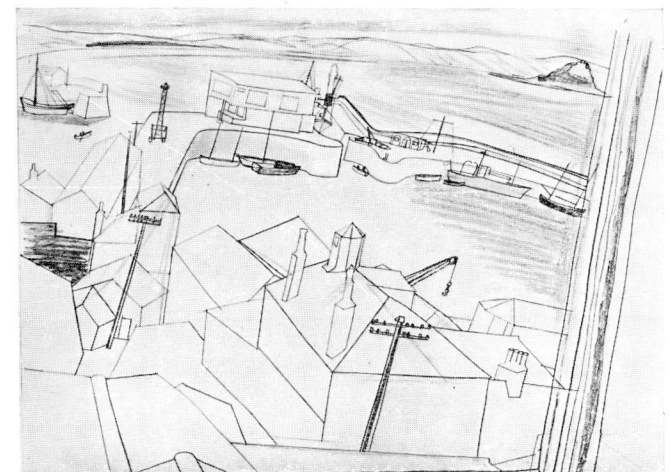

BEN NICHOLSON   *Penzance, inner harbour, June 16–48*

barrier. This language is comprehensible to anyone who doesn't set up barriers—the dog and cat set up no barriers and their eyes, whiskers and tails are alive, without restriction, but the whiskers of an intellectual do not give off the necessary spark and contact cannot be made.

I think that so far from being a limited expression, understood by a few, abstract art is a powerful, unlimited and universal language.

reprinted from "Horizon" October, 1941, with revisions by the author

Within the means of abstract expression there are immense possibilities and it is a language with a power peculiar to itself. But the kind of painting which I find exciting is not necessarily representational or non-representational, but it is both musical and architectural, where the architectural construction is used to express a "musical" relationship between form, tone and colour and whether this visual, "musical", relationship is slightly more or slightly less abstract is for me

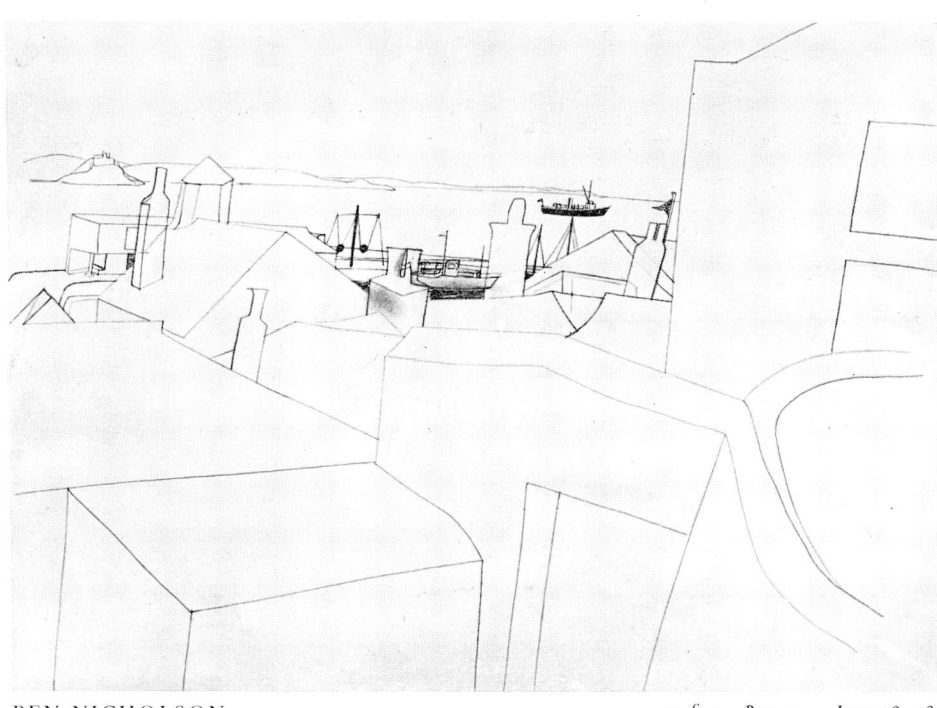

BEN NICHOLSON   *rooftops, Penzance, June 18–48*

beside the point.   1948

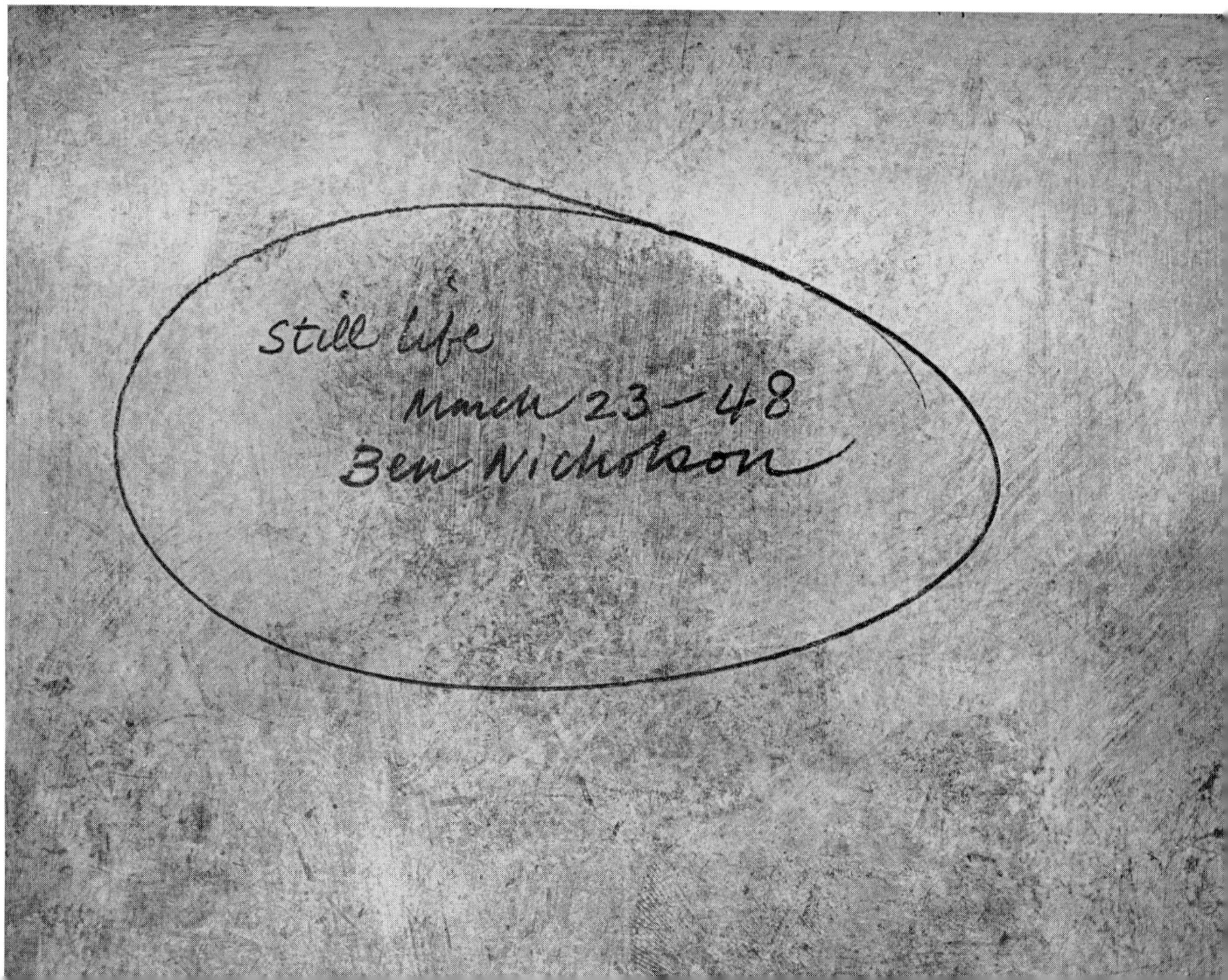

the artist's signature

INTRODUCTION par Herbert Read — résumé

traduite de l'Anglais par Philip Granville

REMARQUONS tout d'abord que la tendance à l'abstraction en art n'est pas l'apanage exclusif de l'art moderne. On la retrouve à maintes reprises au cours de l'histoire de l'art, et elle avait déjà acquis le caractère de phénomène historique sous le nom d'art "abstrait" avant la naissance du mouvement moderne. C'est ainsi que le brillant essai de Wilhelm Worringer intitulé *Abstraktion und Einfühlung*, fut écrit en 1906 et publié en 1908; les caractères distinctifs de l'art abstrait y sont clairement reconnus.

Une des prémisses de mon raisonnement est que le mouvement abstrait en art moderne correspond à un besoin psychologique largement répandu dans le monde d'aujourd'hui; aussi est-il vain de spéculer sur l'importance relative des éléments d'un style moderne abstrait.

Bien que le fameux essai de Worringer n'ait jamais été traduit en Anglais, T. E. Hulme l'a excellemment résumé dans une conférence publiée dans le recueil de ses écrits intitulé *Speculations*.[1] Après avoir parlé de "l'art vital", Hulme, suivant de près le texte de Worringer, écrit:

"Tournons nous maintenant vers l'art géométrique. Il est tout à fait évident que cet art n'exprime pas les joies de la nature ni l'aspiration à la vitalité. Ses formes présentent toujours une apparence raide et inanimée. La forme morte d'une pyramide égyptienne, et l'absence de vie d'une mosaïque byzantine font voir que derrière l'art de ces époques il devait y avoir un motif absolument opposé à celui qui trouve satisfaction dans le naturalisme de l'art grec ou de la Renaissance."

"C'est là ce que Worringer appelle la *Tendance à l'Abstraction*."

"Quelle est la nature de cette tendance? Quel est l'état d'esprit de ceux dont l'art est régi par cette tendance?"

"Elle peut se décrire en termes généraux, comme le sentiment d'une séparation vis-à-vis du monde extérieur."

"Alors que l'art naturaliste exprime une relation panthéiste harmonieuse entre l'homme et le monde extérieur, la tendance à l'abstraction, au contraire, se concentre parmi les races qui ont adopté une attitude diamétralement opposée vis-à-vis du monde extérieur. Ce sentiment de séparation prend naturellement des formes différentes suivant la différence des niveaux de culture."

J'ai déjà suggéré que les théories de Worringer avaient pu inspirer directement les tendances modernes, mais je doute qu'un mouvement ainsi artificiellement commencé eût put acquérir l'importance d'un mouvement universel atteignant tous les arts (car la musique d'un compositeur comme Schönberg s'y rattache aussi bien que la tendance générale de l'architecture moderne), si le besoin caché et impérieux de ce mode d'expression ne se fût fait sentir. En fait, depuis de nombreuses années, la philosophie préparait le terrain à un tel développement, et au "Raumscheu", l'inquiétude spatiale de Worringer, correspond l'"Angst", l'anxiété de Heidegger, qui n'est autre qu'une inquiétude spatiale, une peur du néant aux dimensions cosmiques.

Worringer et Hulme ont reconnu la coexistence, dans le passé, de styles abstrait et naturaliste. Mais les conditions sociales et psychologiques sont traitées comme des expressions collectives, nées d'un groupe ou d'une classe particulière. Il nous faut affirmer à présent la possibilité, non seulement d'une réaction individuelle, mais même de l'alternance de deux attitudes au sein de la conscience individuelle. En s'en tenant à la surface des choses, cette possibilité peut s'interpréter simplement comme l'alternance de moments optimistes et pessimistes. Si même l'on admet l'analyse existentialiste de la position de l'homme dans l'univers, il reste encore à l'individu la possibilité de réagir positivement ou négativement, avec désespoir ou avec courage, avec crainte ou avec confiance. Dans certains cas il semble que l'individu puisse passer de l'un à l'autre des extrêmes représentés par ces deux pôles, tendant au cours d'une phase psychologique, vers une affirmation du monde, d'où le style naturaliste—et, au cours d'une autre, vers un rejet du monde, d'où un style abstrait. Ben Nicholson est un artiste qui appartient à ce type complexe.

II

C'est introduire aussitôt un paradoxe que de décrire Ben Nicholson comme un artiste "complexe", car aucun artiste n'est à un plus haut degré exempt de l'introspection égocentrique que suggère l'idée de complexité. Pour lui, l'art a été un processus continuel d'exploration et de découverte, et la conquête de chaque nouveau territoire a servi de point de départ à une nouvelle expédition. Il appelle souvent ces découvertes, des "idées", mais une idée est pour lui quelque chose "sur quoi on peut travailler", un matériau concret de sensation à pétrir et à façonner sensuellement. Certains symboles restent constants: la cruche du tableau ingénu de 1911 (planche 1) réapparaît continuellement, et figure parmi les dernières œuvres de 1947-8. Les couleurs franches et gaies des fruits, des cartes à jouer, des bouchons de canne à pêche et des poteries vernissées, sont également des facteurs invariables. Le clair-obscur est éliminé

---

[1] Londres, 1924, Kegan Paul, pp. 75-109

ou maintenu dans des limites précises comme dans une mosaïque byzantine. Cependant l'artiste, au moyen de ces facteurs identiques à eux-mêmes, crée des variations infinies et, sans réflexion préconçue, tout naturellement, il parvient aux pôles opposés du réalisme et de l'abstraction.

Les abstractions ne proviennent nullement d'un sujet donné, et celui-ci n'est pas imposé davantage sur une construction architecturale prédéterminée (a là manière de Juan Gris). Il arrive que les relations formelles émergent du monde objectif, telles les représentations sommaires des murs, fenêtres et portes de la Ville de Halse (planche 109); parfois aussi quelque chose de très proche—au sens géométrique étroit—se répète dans une abstraction, tel l'exemple de la planche 110. Mais les similitudes sont dues principalement aux limites qu'imposent les formules géométriques dont l'artiste se libère rarement (les planches 25 et 26 marquent les bornes d'une semblable liberté, et sont pour cette raison exceptionnelles).

La simplicité et le petit nombre de symboles formels employés par cet artiste ne constituent pas une limitation de sa puissance inventive; il s'abandonne au contraire avec joie à la multiplicité des variations que lui offrent ces moyens restreints et, comme tous les grands artistes, il sait que la beauté résulte de difficultés que l'on s'impose à soi-même.

On peut penser que l'art de Ben Nicholson donne prise à l'accusation d'être un art *Purement Décoratif*. Outre qu'il est vrai, comme l'a affirmé Ruskin, que tout art est décoratif dans la mesure où il est art, il est certain que la peinture de Ben Nicholson n'est pas même décorative au sens péjoratif du mot. Employé dans ce sens, "décoratif" sert à décrire des motifs à deux dimensions entièrement dénués de substance. Mais comme le fait remarquer Henri Focillon, "la forme a un sens, mais qui est tout d'elle, une valeur personnelle et particulière qu'il ne faut pas confondre avec les attributs qu'on lui impose".[2]

Suivant cette conception, les valeurs formelles des peintures de Ben Nicholson valent celles des formes de Poussin ou de Rembrandt ou de Cézanne. Ce sont des constructions matérielles à trois dimensions, dotées de tous les éléments de semblables constructions: rythme, équilibre, clair-obscur et réalité positive.

III

L'art est variété; l'art est aventure.

Ce serait présomption que de porter un jugement sur un peintre don't l'activité ne s'est pas encore relantie; cependant, comme le montre bien ce volume, son œuvre est déjà considérable, et la continuité dont elle fait preuve, ce qu'elle révèle d'une sensibilité sans défaut, la variété des formes qui jaillissent d'une source qu'on dirait intarissable, tout cela nous fait reconnaître en Ben Nicholson un des grands artistes de notre temps. Apollinaire a écrit:

"Les grands poètes et les grands artistes ont pour fonction sociale de renouveler sans cesse l'apparence que revêt la nature aux yeux des hommes. Sans les poètes, sans les artistes les hommes s'ennuieraient vite de la monotonie naturelle."[3]

L'œuvre de Ben Nicholson est particulièrement significative en ce qu'avec des moyens relativement simples et directs, elle suscite les vibrations les plus intenses de la sensibilité esthétique.

---

[2] Henri Focillon, *Vie des Formes*, Librairie Ernest Leroux, Paris 1934, page 4

[3] *Les Peintres Cubistes*, Paris, 1913

DE L'ART "ABSTRAIT"

Notes de Ben Nicholson *traduites de l'Anglais par Philip Granville*

A PROPOS de l'art abstrait: je ne me suis pas encore aperçu que l'on ait remarqué que cette libération de la forme et de la couleur est étroitement liée aux autres libérations dont on entend parler. Peut-être devrait-elle faire partie de nos buts de guerre. Après tout, chaque mouvement de la vie humaine est affecté par la forme et la couleur; tout ce que nous voyons, touchons ou sentons y est lié, de sorte que l'usage qu'un artiste peut faire librement et de façon créatrice de ces éléments peut avoir sur nos vies une influence d'une puissance formidable. Par exemple la capacité de créer l'espace (non pas l'espace littéraire mais l'espace réel) est d'une valeur inestimable. Loin d'être pour l'artiste une "tour d'ivoire" où il peut se réfugier contre le réalité, l'art "abstrait" a une fois de plus ramené l'art dans le domaine de la vie quotidienne. La preuve en est dans sa parenté spirituelle et son influence sur l'architecture contemporaine, les avions, les automobiles, les frigorifiques, la typographie, la publicité, les lampes électriques, les étuis de rouge à lèvres, etc. Mais de même que les plus profondes des idées religieuses, scientifiques, musicales et artistiques, son message fondamental n'est compris que de quelques rares personnes qui, semble-t-il, le transmettent de proche en proche jusqu'à ce qu'il atteigne le reste du monde qui l'incorporera inconsciemment à sa vie. Un Raphaël n'est pas une peinture de la National Gallery—c'est une force vive de notre existence.

C'est interessant que lors d'une exposition d'art abstrait tenue par moi à Londres, des personnes de professions variées m'ont écrit qu'elles avaient le sentiment d'un lien entre leur métier et le mien: c'est ainsi qu'un constructeur de yachts m'a dit que ce qui fait qu'un bateau file ou qu'un bateau peine, c'est l'exactitude du dessin à un cheveu près, et qu'il lui semblait qu'elle aussi décidât de la puissance ou de la faiblesse d'un relief. Ces correspondants pénétraient le problème mieux que les critiques préoccupés de savoir s'il s'agissait d'œuvres d'art, et se demandant pourquoi (à première vue) elles ressemblaient alors si peu à des Tintoret. On peut dire que les problèmes dont traite l'art "abstrait" sont liés à des jeux de forces et, par conséquent, que toute solution à laquelle on s'arrête exerce une influence sur tout jeu de forces, qu'il s'agisse d'un match entre l'Arsenal at le Racing ou du mouvement des astres. Je pense que la libération récente des forces de la forme et de la couleur est un événement important, et lorsque les critiques annoncent ou prédisent la mort de l'art abstrait, ils méconnaissent la liberté de la forme et de la couleur tout comme les dictateurs méconnaissent celle de l'individu: toutefois une entreprise visant à mettre fin à l'une ou à l'autre est vouée à l'echec dès le départ; car elle n'a pas d'autre choix: mettre fin à la race humaine ainsi qu'à toute autre forme de vie.

Beaucoup de peintures et de sculptures contemporaines se dirigent vers l'imitation d'un homme, d'un arbre ou d'une fleur au lieu de se servir de la couleur et de la forme pour créer *l'equivalent* de ceux-ci; personne ne demandera ce qu'un arbre est censé représenter et pourtant, avec la plus parfaite innocence on demandera ce qu'une peinture ou une sculpture ou une construction dans l'espace sont censés représenter. Il faut concevoir cet équivalent dans les limites de la technique employée; il faut qu'il soit une expression picturale et sculpturale pure, car l'introduction d'un élément étranger signifie que la conception est faussée et ne peut plus par conséquent s'appliquer complètement à d'autres formes de vie.

Une des différences principales entre une peinture figurative et une peinture abstraite est que la première peut vous transporter en Grèce en représentant une mer et un ciel bleu, des oliviers et des colonnes de marbre, à condition de vous concentrer sur le tableau si vous voulez participer au spectacle. Au contraire la version abstraite, en employant librement forme et couleur, vous apportera la quintessence de la Grèce, et deviendra ainsi une part de la lumière, de l'espace et de la vie dans la pièce—l'effort de concentration n'est plus nécessaire et ne fera qu'un avec la vie.

Quand on peint une "nature morte" on prend pour base de l'expression d'une idée les formes simples de tous les jours, bouteille-pot-cruche-assiette-sur-table: les formes ne sont pas entièrement libres bien qu'elles soient libres dans la mesure où chaque objet peut être vu d'autant de points de vue que l'on désire à un même moment mais les couleurs sont libres: couleur bouteille pour l'assiette, couleur assiette pour la table, ou n'importe qu'elle autre que l'on puisse souhaiter; en travaillant dans ce sens, on n'a plus au bout d'un certain temps une nature morte d'objets, mais quelque chose d'équivalent ressemblant plutôt à des daims passant à travers une forêt l'hiver, par delà les collines et les montagnes, à travers la lumière et les ombres de l'Arizona, de la Cornouailles ou de la Provence; ainsi, inévitablement, il arrive un moment où l'on rejette complètement les formes des objets même les plus simples qui servaient de base et où l'on sort son idée, non seulement en couleurs libres mais aussi en formes libres. Ce développement doit sembler simple à la plupart des gens, mais, par exemple dans mon cas bien que je fis ma première peinture "abstraite" en 1923 ce n'est qu'en 1933 que je fus capable d'établir fermement ce développement. Au début je traçai des cercles en me laissant aller à ma fantaisie et j'assemblai au hasard les éléments de mes constructions: plus tard, j'attachai davantage de valeur au contact direct que je pouvais obtenir au moyen de plans colorés plats, exécutés et réglés avec la rigueur d'un accord parfait, ainsi qu'à la tension accrue obtenue au moyen de cercles parfaits et de rectangles; ainsi l'idée perdit en séduction ce qu'elle gagna en force, et son impact devint plus direct et plus puissant.

Les formes géométriques employées par les artistes de l'école abstraite n'indiquent pas, comme on le croit généralement, un processus conscient, intellectuel et mathématique; un carré ou un cercle en art ne sont rien en eux-mêmes et ne vivent que de l'emploi instinctif et inspiré qu'un artiste peut en faire en exprimant une idée poétique. Si l'on prend un grand carré bleu d'outremer et un petit carré rouge de cadmium et qu'on les dispose sur une surface blanche froide auprès d'un cercle tracé au crayon, on provoque une tension entre ces forces; mais que cette tension devienne trop forte il est facile, en marquant du compas le centre du cercle de le percer tout simplement comme un papillon!

Récemment dans *Horizon*, Graham Greene a parlé dans un article sur Read d'une "décoration de fils de fer et de petites boules oscillantes suspendue au plafond". A son avis c'est là une nouvelle mode, étrange et sans aucun rapport avec l'art. Je me trouvai un jour à Paris devant un Calder (comme celui-ci); je l'empruntai et le suspendis au centre du plafond d'une pièce blanche ayant vue sur la Seine et le soir, face au fleuve miroitant, le mobile tournait lentement dans la brise à la lumière d'une ampoule électrique suspendue vers son centre—une grande boule noire, cinq petites boules blanches et une petite boule écarlate tournant lentement au bout de fils de fer, autour, au-dessus et au-dessous l'une de l'autre, leurs ombres se poursuivant autour des murs blancs en un mouvement interdépendant passionnant, accélérant soudain dans les angles et disparaissant dans la nuit en passant par la fenêtre: c'était vivant comme le bourdonnement de la ville, comme le fleuve qui coulait et comme l'odeur de Paris au début du printemps; cependant ce n'était pas une œuvre d'art comme on l'entend d'ordinaire—emprisonnée dans une cadre doré ou dressée inanimée sur un piedestal dans un de nos mausolées aux colonnes de marbre. Mais c'était "vivant", ce qui n'est pas mal après tout pour une œuvre d'art.

De la construction dans l'espace je puis montrer un aspect à l'aide d'une de mes peintures du début: une devanture de magasin à Dieppe (*planche 58*), quoi qu'a ce moment là il ne m'était pas venu à l'esprit de m'occuper de la notion d'espace, employant tout simplement la devanture comme un thème sur lequel je

pouvais baser mon idée. Le magasin s'appelait "Au Chat Botté", ce qui fit naître en moi un flot d'idées associées aux contes de fées de mon enfance; en outre mon français étant plutôt étrange ces mots mêmes acquéraient un caractère abstrait. Mais ce qui l'emportait c'était le nom imprimé en très belles lettres rouges sur la vitrine du magasin, *constituant ainsi un premier plan*—et le reflet sur la fenêtre de ce qui se trouvait derrière moi pendant que je regardais à l'intérieur, *constituant un second plan*—tandis que dans le magasin des objets placés sur une table exécutaient une sorte de ballet formant l'"œil" ou centre vital de la peinture, *constituant un troisième plan*. Ces trois plans et tous leurs plans auxiliaires étaient interchangeables, de sorte que l'on ne pouvait distinguer ce qui était réel de ce qui était irréel, ni ce qui était réfléchi de ce qui n'était pas réfléchi. Il en résultait, je le vois à présent, pour ainsi dire un espace ou un monde de l'imagination où l'on pouvait vivre.

On se trouve en face du même processus lorsque l'on exécute une peinture ou un relief abstrait; pour donner un exemple simple, prenons une surface rectangulaire et découpons-en une partie dans un plan inférieur; puis dans le plan supérieur découpons un cercle plus profond et ne touchant pas le plan inférieur. *On est aussitôt conscient que ce cercle a percé le plan inférieur sans l'avoir touché*—un chien ou un chat eux-mêmes s'en rendraient compte instantanément—et c'est cela qui crée l'espace. Cette connaissance est ressentie dans le subconscient et il est vain de l'aborder intellectuellement car cette attitude, loin d'aider, ne fait que dresser une barrière. Quiconque n'élève pas de barrières peut comprendre cette langue—le chien et le chat n'élèvent pas de barrières et leurs yeux, leurs moustaches, leurs queues vibrent sans contrainte mais les moustaches d'un intellectuel ne produisent pas l'étincelle voulue et le contact ne se fait pas.

Je pense que loin d'être une expression limitée et comprise par peu de gens, l'art abstrait est une langue puissante, sans limites et universelle.

réimpression de "Horizon", octobre 1941, révisée par l'auteur

Les moyens de l'expression abstraite offrent des possibilités illimitées et c'est une langue douée d'une puissance et d'une étendue propre; cependant le genre de peinture que je trouve stimulant n'est pas nécessairement lié soit à la représentation, soit à l'absence de représentation mais il est à la fois musical et architectural, la construction architecturale servant à exprimer un rapport "musical" entre forme, ton et couleur, bien que le degré d'abstraction de ce rapport visuel, "musical", ne m'importe peu.

juin 1948

collection William Nicholson

1 striped jug 1911

collection H. S. Ede

2 still life (Balearic Islands) 1925

3 *Bré Ticino 1921*

collection Winifred Nicholson

4 *still life, Villa Capriccio, Castagnola 1921–22*

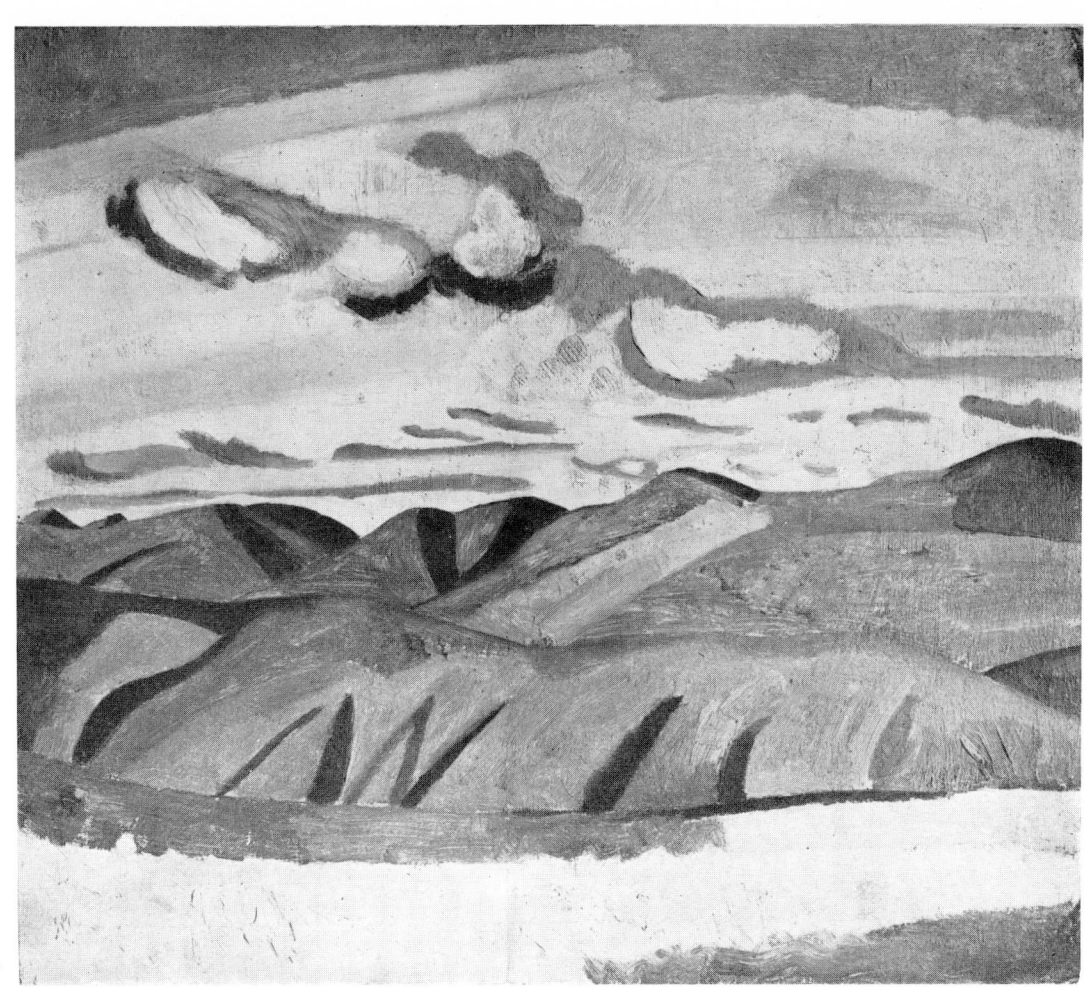

5 *coast of Spain c. 1922–23*

6 *Cortivallo, Lugano 1921*   collection Winifred Nicholson

bottle and goblet
c. 1924

7

collection H. S. Ede

goblet and two pears
1924

8

collection C. S. Reddihough
9 painting (trout) 1924

(destroyed)
10 painting c. 1923–24

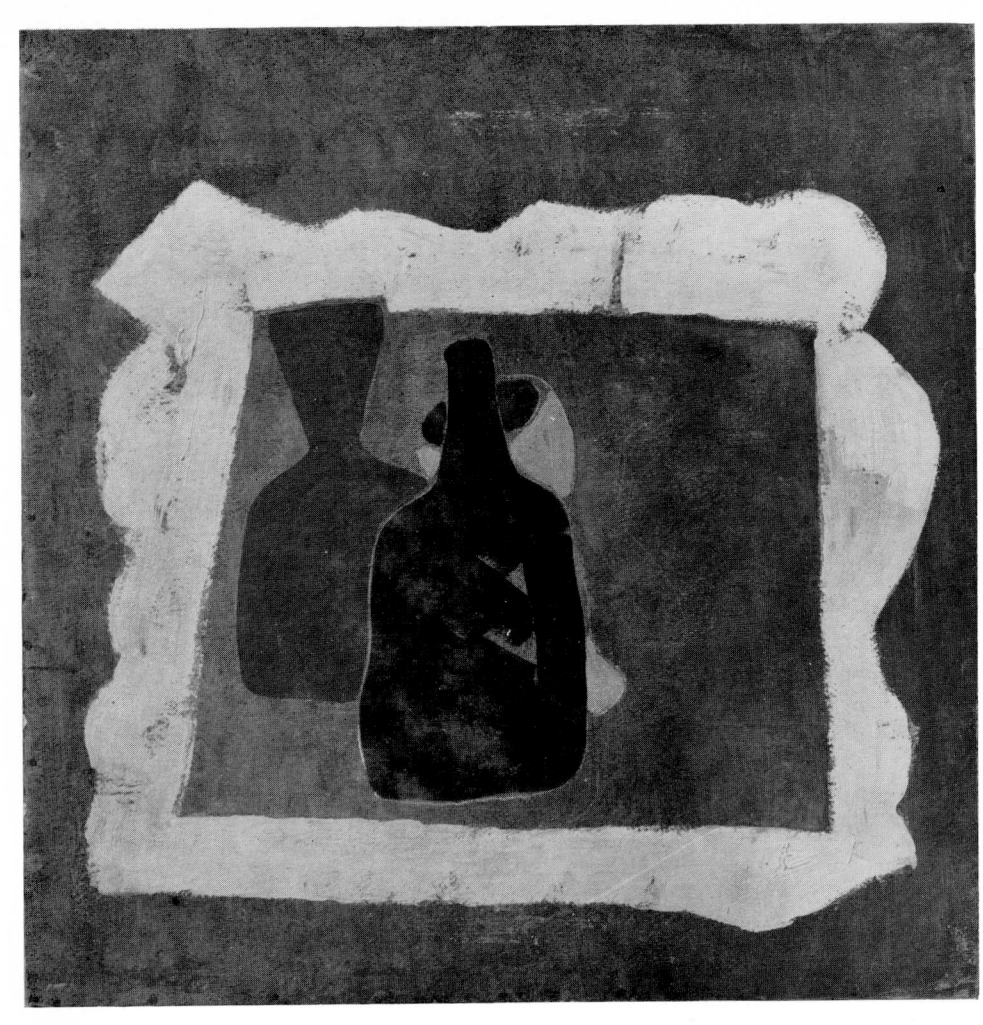

(destroyed)

11 *still life 1926*

version 1 collection Helen Sutherland (illustrated)
version 2 collection The British Council

12 *still life with fruit 1926*

13 *still life* (L.L.) *1926*   collection W. Staite Murray

collection E. J. Hooper

14 *flowers* c. *1927*

15 *still life with knife and lemon 1927*   collection H. S. Ede

16 *still life with fruit 1927*   collection F. L. S. Murray

17 *Le Quotidien* 1934   collection F. L. S. Murray

18 *still life* 1930   collection H. S. Ede

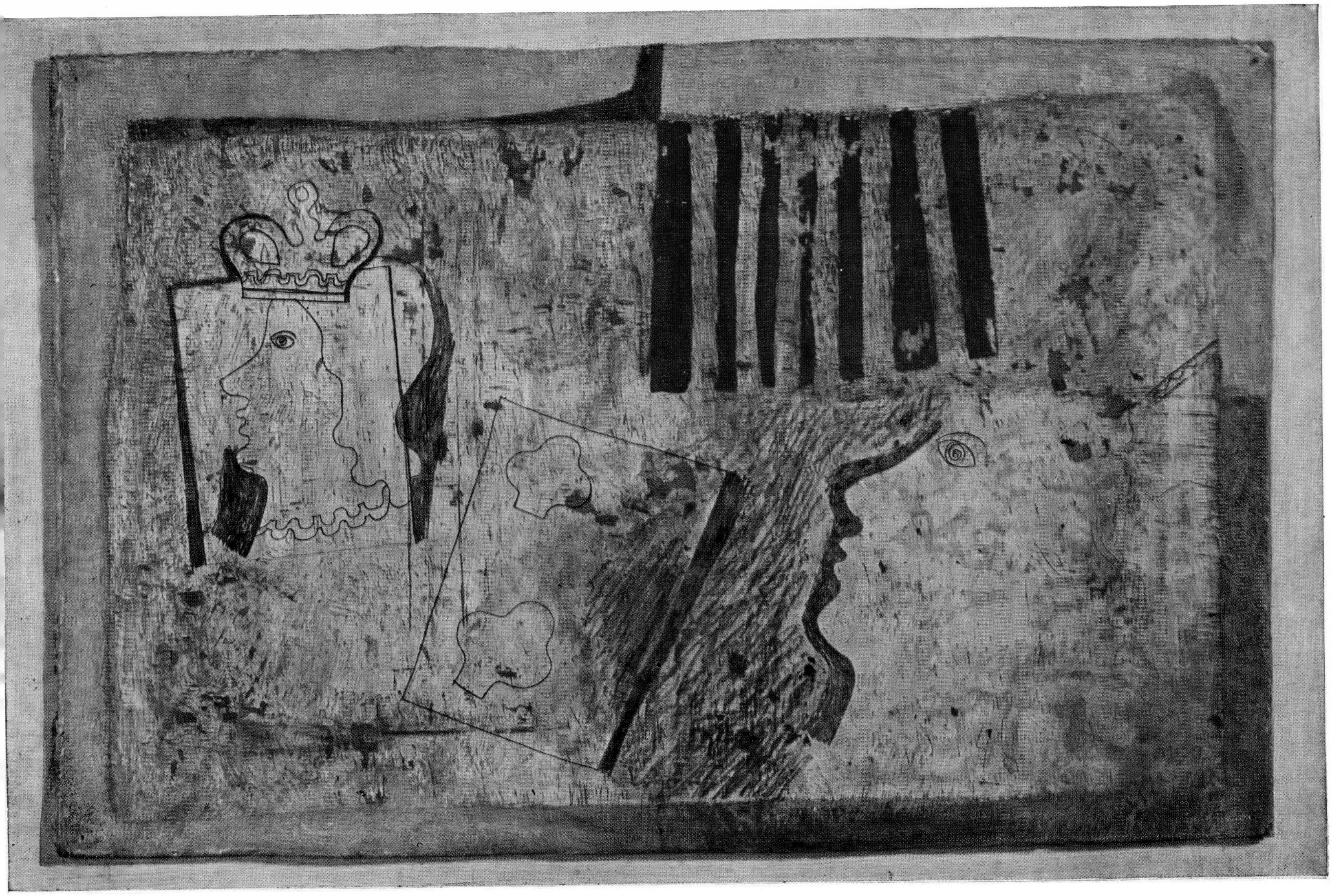

19 *prince and princess 1932*   collection John Summerson

20 *still life with pear 1931–32*   collection F. L. S. Murray

collection
Helen Sutherland

1929
pomegranate

21

collection Barbara Hepworth

1930
prince and princess

22

(destroyed)
c. 1929
Cumbrian farm

23

collection H. S. Ede

Cornish port c. 1930

24

collection H. S. Ede

Cumbrian landscape c. 1928

25

26 *apples c. 1927*   collection H. S. Ede

27 *Porthmeor beach, St. Ives 1928*

collection Helen Sutherland

28 *still life* c. 1927   collection W. P. Barratt

29 *flowers* c. 1924–25   collection Helen Sutherland

30 *breakfast table, Banks Head–Villa Capriccio c. 1928*   collection Helen Sutherland

31 *Cumbrian landscape* (version 1) *1928* collection Helen Sutherland

32 *Pill Creek, Cornwall 1928*   collection C. S. Reddihough

33 *profile* (Venetian red) *1932*   collection H. S. Ede

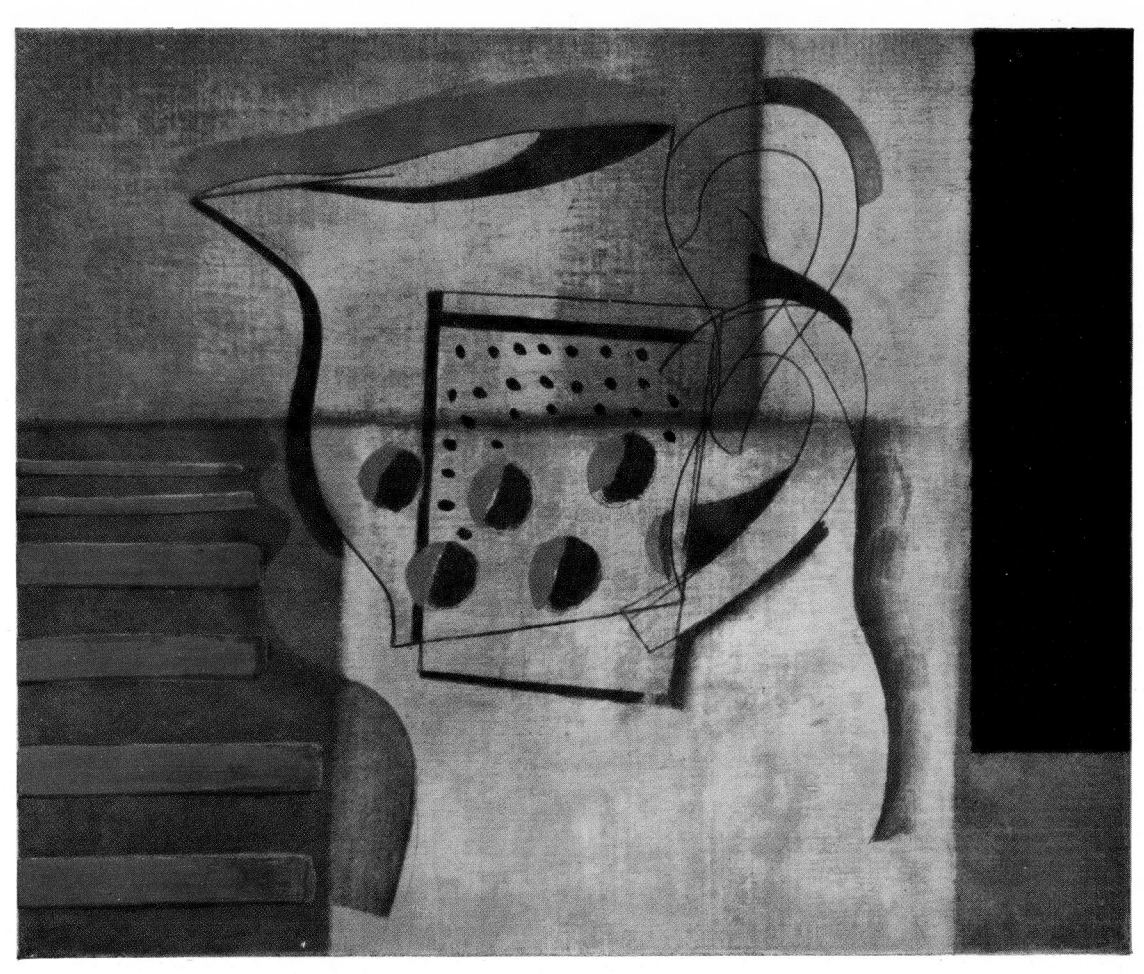

collection J. C. Pritchard
34 *still life 1932*

collection C. S. Reddihough
35 *still life 1929–35*

36 *still life* (Mediterranean) *1933*   collection Adrian Stokes

37 *St. Remy, Provence 1932*   *collection Barbara Hepworth*

38 *two diamonds 1929*

39 *Cumbrian landscape* (version 2) *1928*   collection Wilfred Roberts

collection E. and D. Noyes

frostbound (Cumberland) c. 1927–28

40

41 *girl in mirror 1933*   collection H. Honda

42 *still life 1933–35*   collection Helen Sutherland

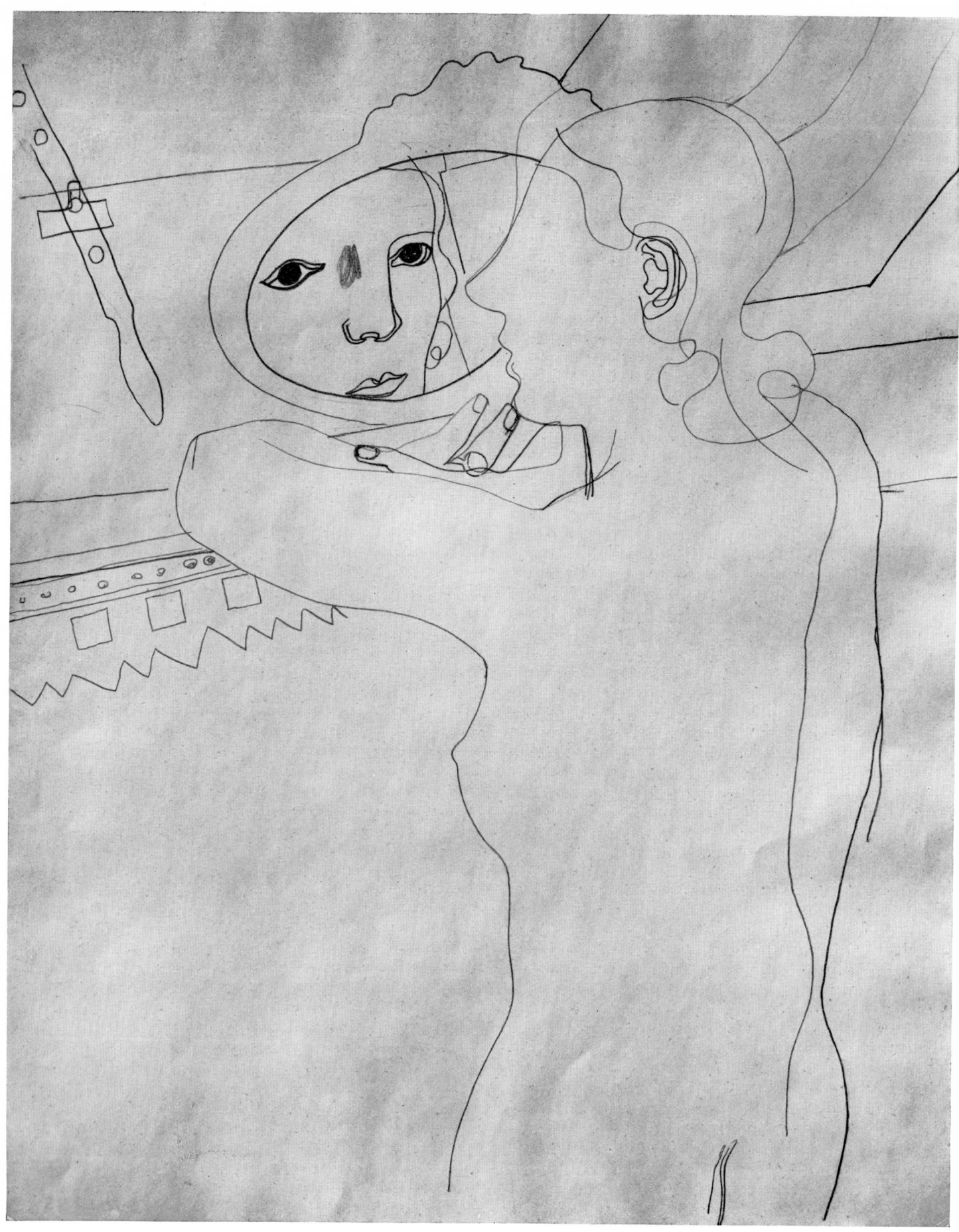

43 *girl in mirror 1932* collection Helen Sutherland

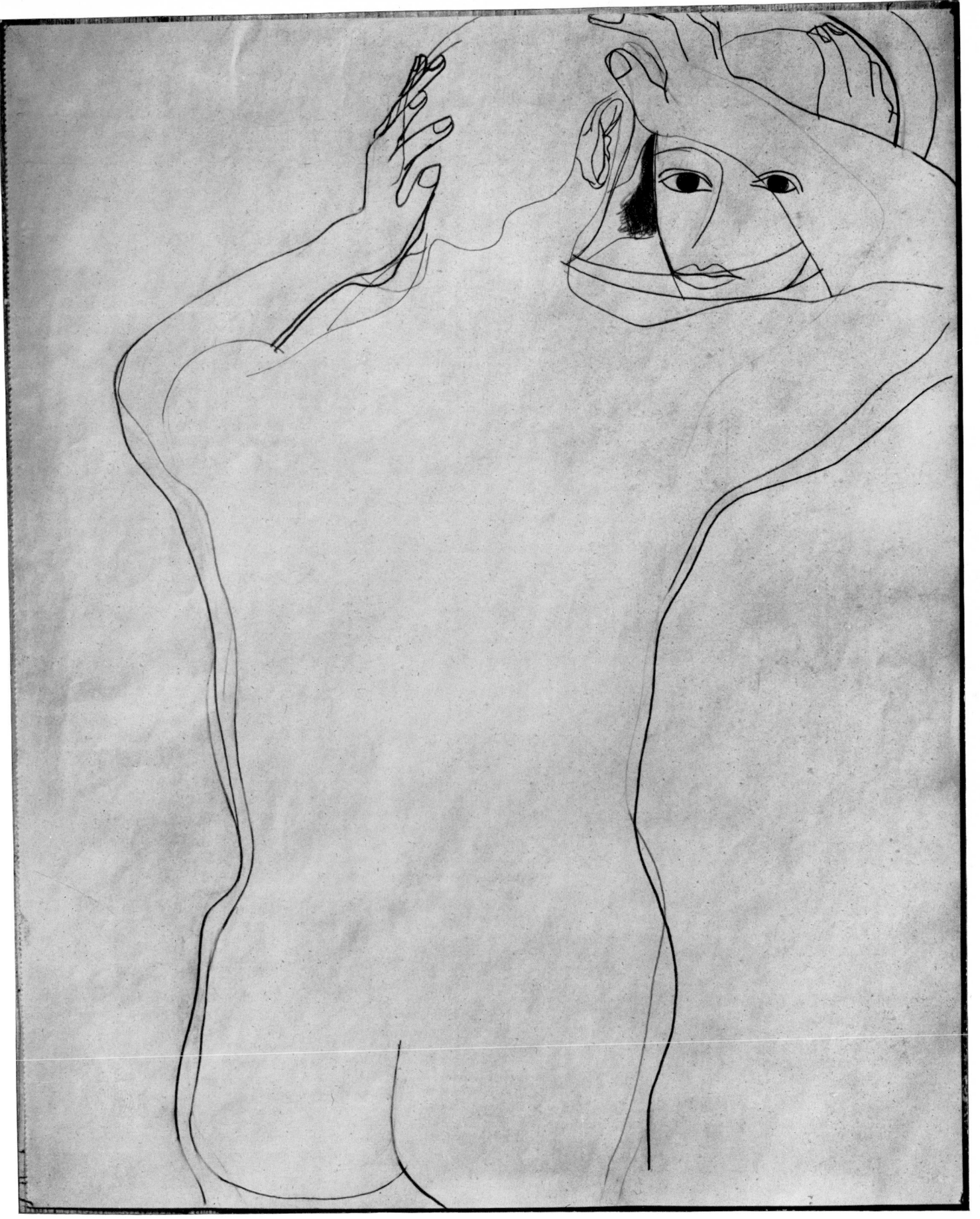

44 *girl in mirror 1932*   collection J. R .M. Brumwell

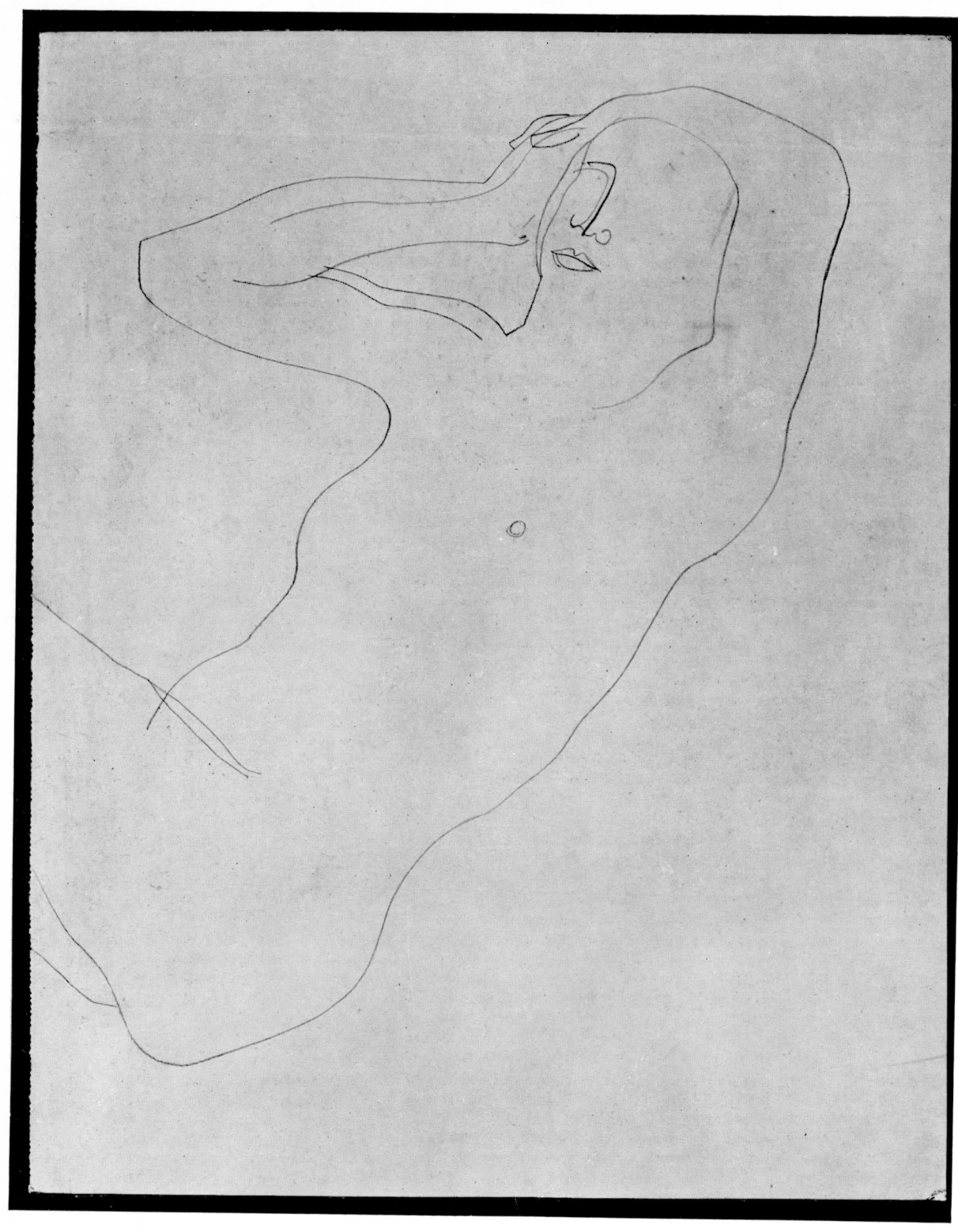

45 *nude 1932*

46 *Seine, Paris c. 1932–33*

Kate, Paris c. 1933

47

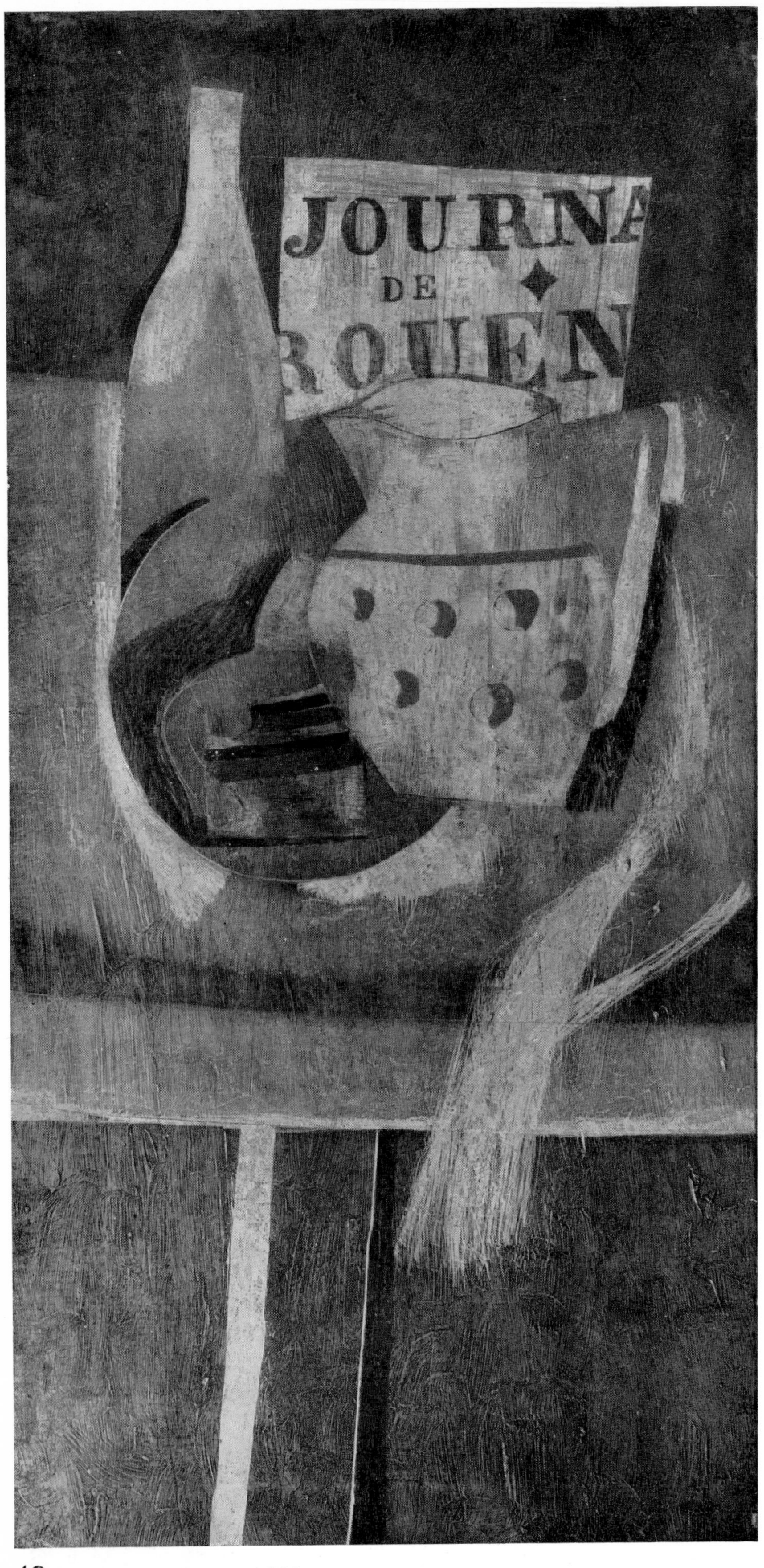

48 *Journal de Rouen 1932*

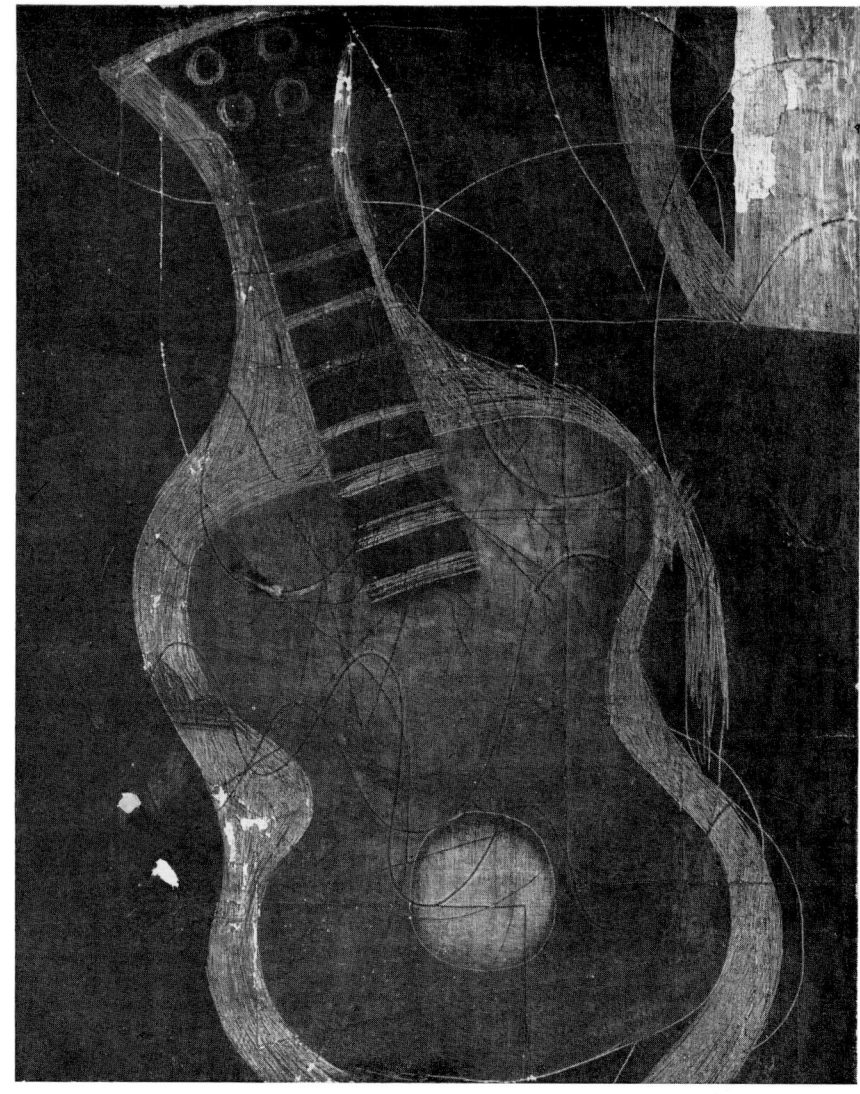

49 *guitar 1933* collection H. S. Ede

50 *painting 1933* collection Whitney Straight

Pont Royal, Paris c. 1932–33

51

collection E. O. Nicholson

still life 1932

52

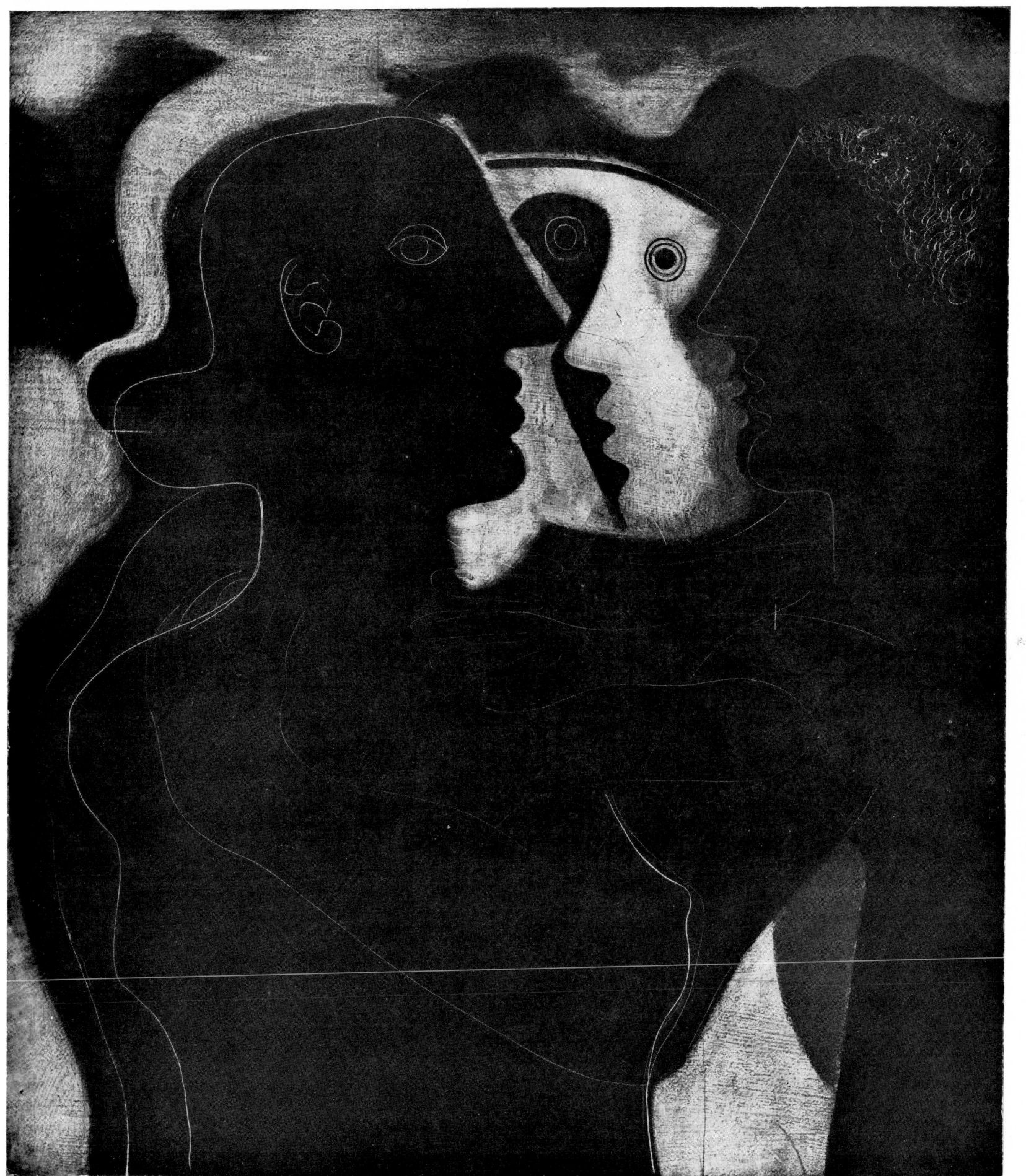

53 *St. Remy, Provence 1933* *collection Helen Sutherland*

54 *playing cards 1932*   *collection Geoffrey Grigson*

55 *painted relief December 1933* (first relief)
collection Winifred Nicholson

56 *six circles 1933*   collection Winifred Nicholson

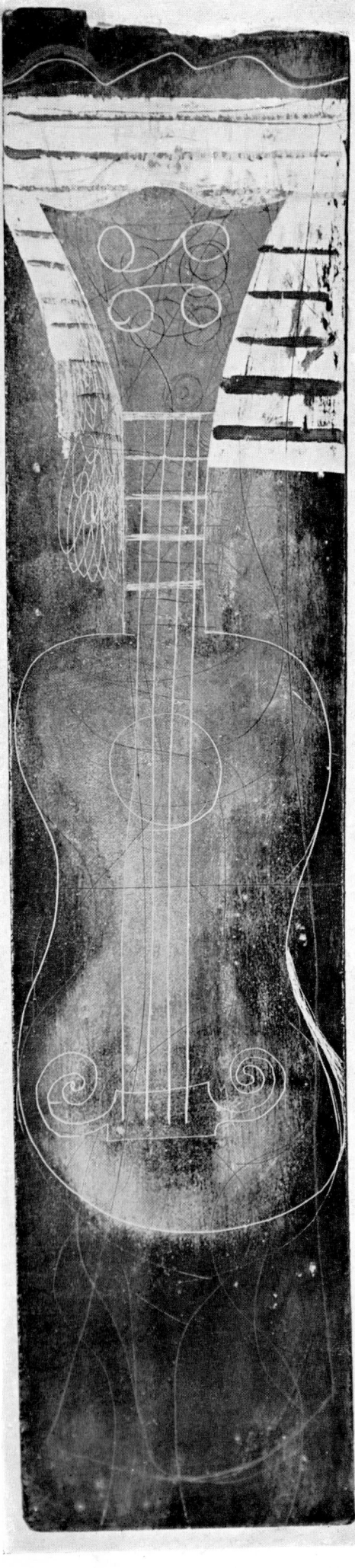

58 *Au Chat Botté* 1932
collection Manchester City Art Gallery

59 *painting* 1933
collection Edna Nixon

57 *guitar* 1933   *collection Tate Gallery*

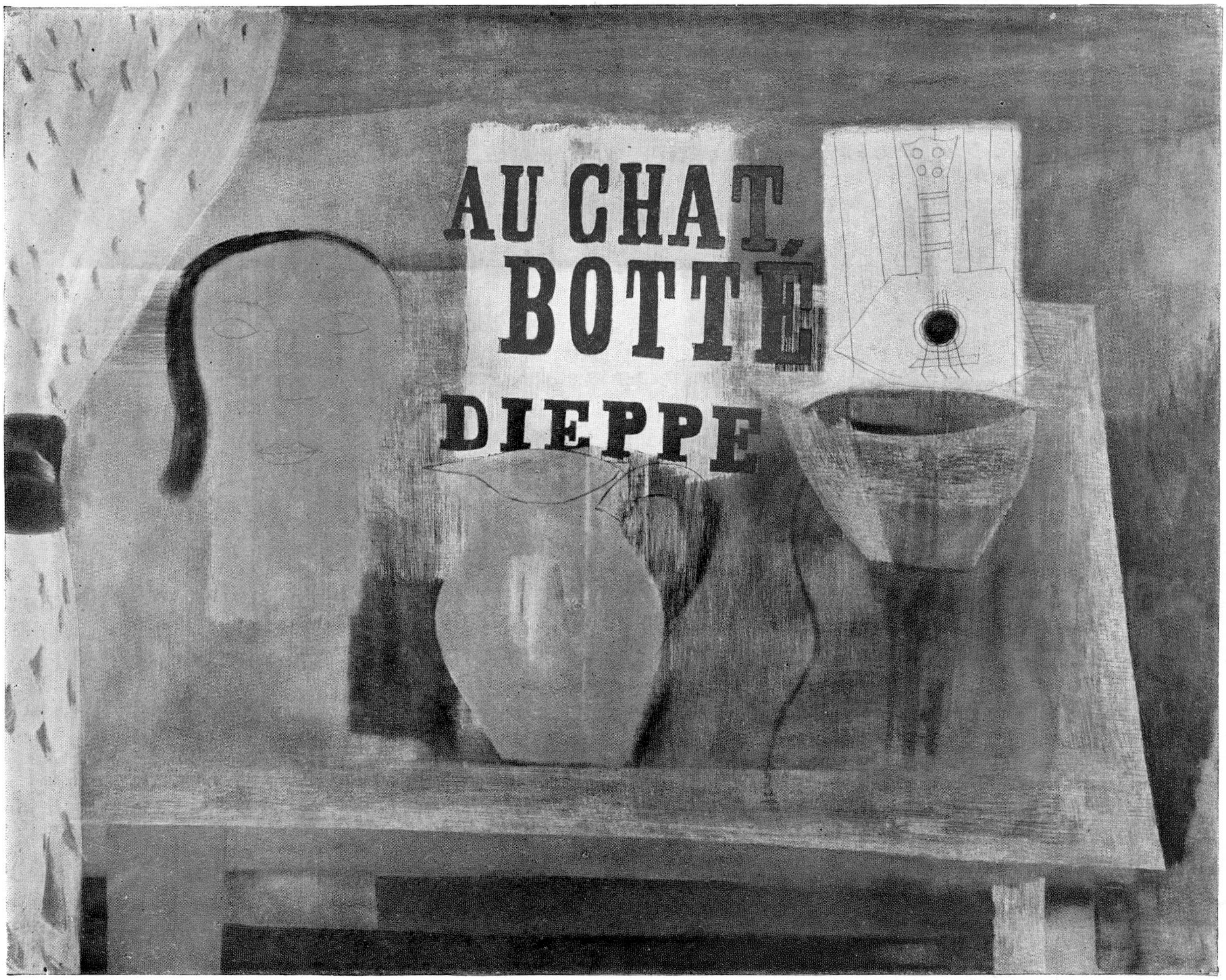
AU CHAT, BOTTÉ
DIEPPE

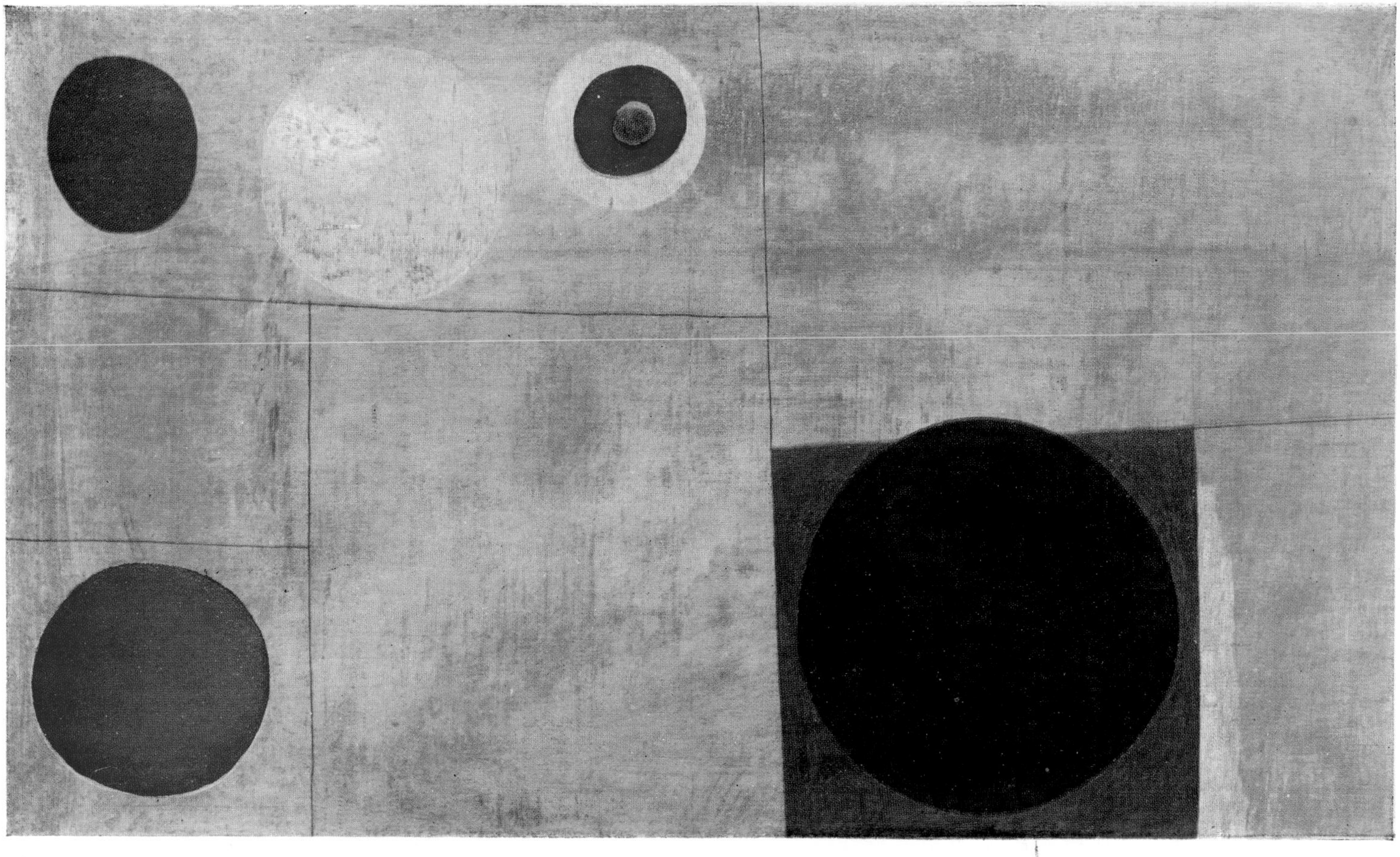

60 *act-drop curtain for Beethoven 7th Symphony ballet 1934*   (designed for L. Massine)   collection S. and J. L. Martin

61 *sketch for 7th Symphony ballet 1934*   collection H. S. Ede

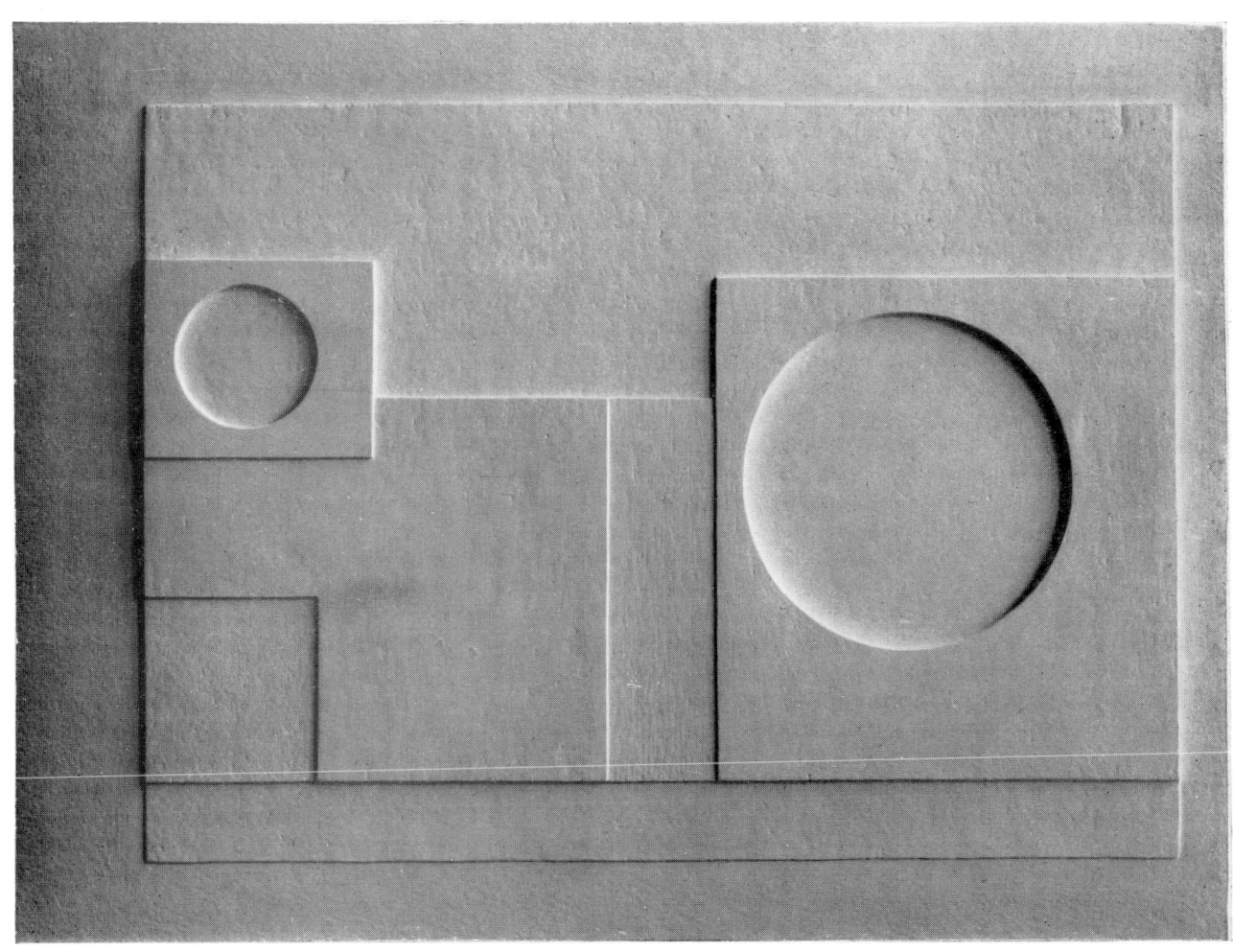

62 *décor for 7th Symphony ballet* (4th movement) *version 1939*

version 1   collection S. and J. L. Martin (illustrated)
project   collection Elizabeth and John Summerson
version 2   collection Serge Chermayeff

63 *Auberge de la Sole Dieppoise 1932*   *collection Jenny Nicholson*

63a *two fishes* (Rouen) *1932*   collection Redfern Gallery

63b *two heads 1932*   collection Barbara Hepworth

64 painting (hibiscus) 1933

65 *painting 1933*

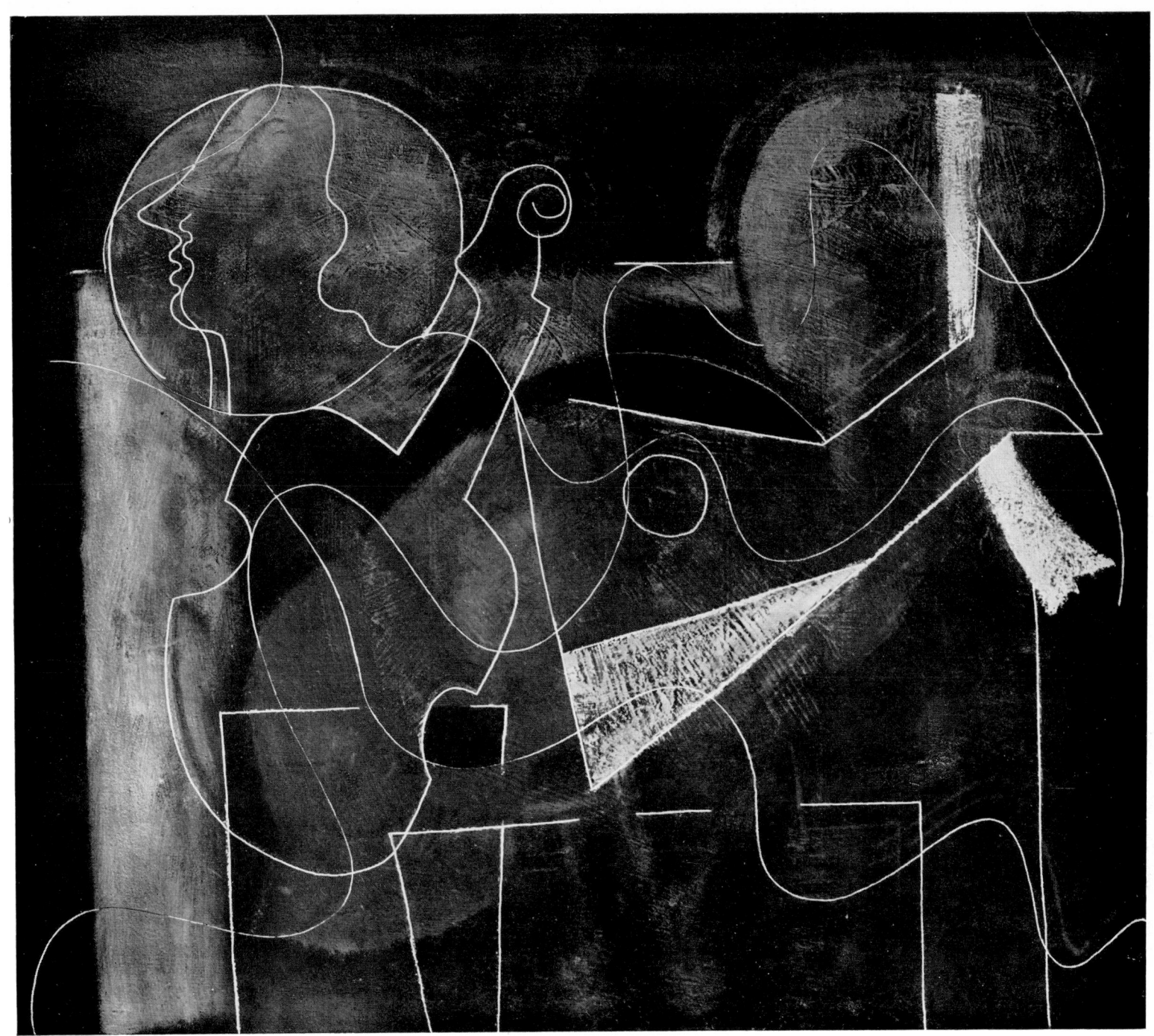

66 *coin and musical instruments 1933*

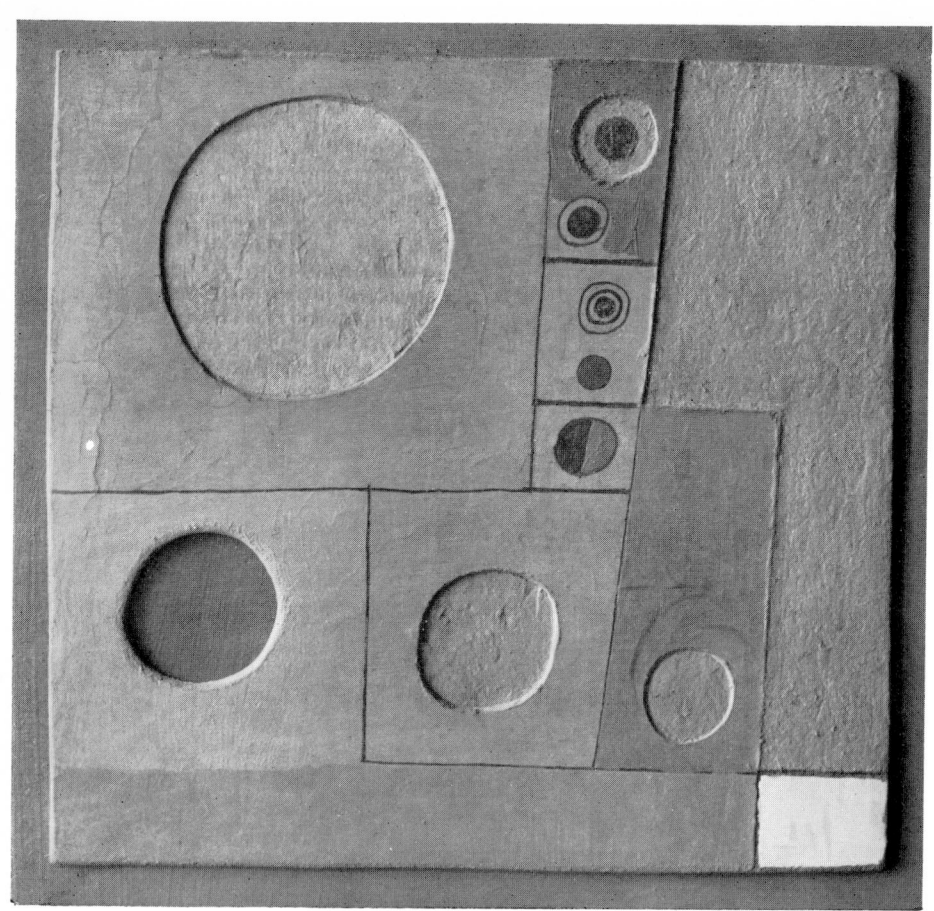

67 *project 1934*   collection John Wells

68 *still life 1934*   collection F. L. S. Murray

69 *white relief 1934* collection Herbert Read

70 *relief 1934* collection the late Hans Frankfort

71 *white relief 1938*   collection the late E. McKnight Kauffer

72 *painting 1937*

73 *painting 1937*   version 1   collection S. and J. L. Martin (illustrated)
version 2   collection J. D. H. Catleugh

74 *painting 1938*   version 1   (illustrated)
                          version 2   collection Alexander Calder

75 *painting 1938*   collection John Summerson

version 1   collection E. H. Ramsden (illustrated)
version 2   collection Adrian Stokes

76 *painting 1942*

still life (Bocquet) *1932*

78 *still life* (Italian) *1934* collection F. L. S. Murray

79 *white relief 1934* collection S. and J. L. Martin

80 *white relief* (triplets) *October 2 1934*

81 *painting 1935* collection S. and J. L. Martin

82 *painting* (Florentine ballet) *1934* collection S. and J. L. Martin

83 *painting* (cadmium red, lemon and cerulean) *1936*

84 *white relief* (*quai d'Auteuil*) *1935*   collection Winifred Nicholson

85 *painted relief* (plover's egg blue) *1940*   collection Helen Sutherland

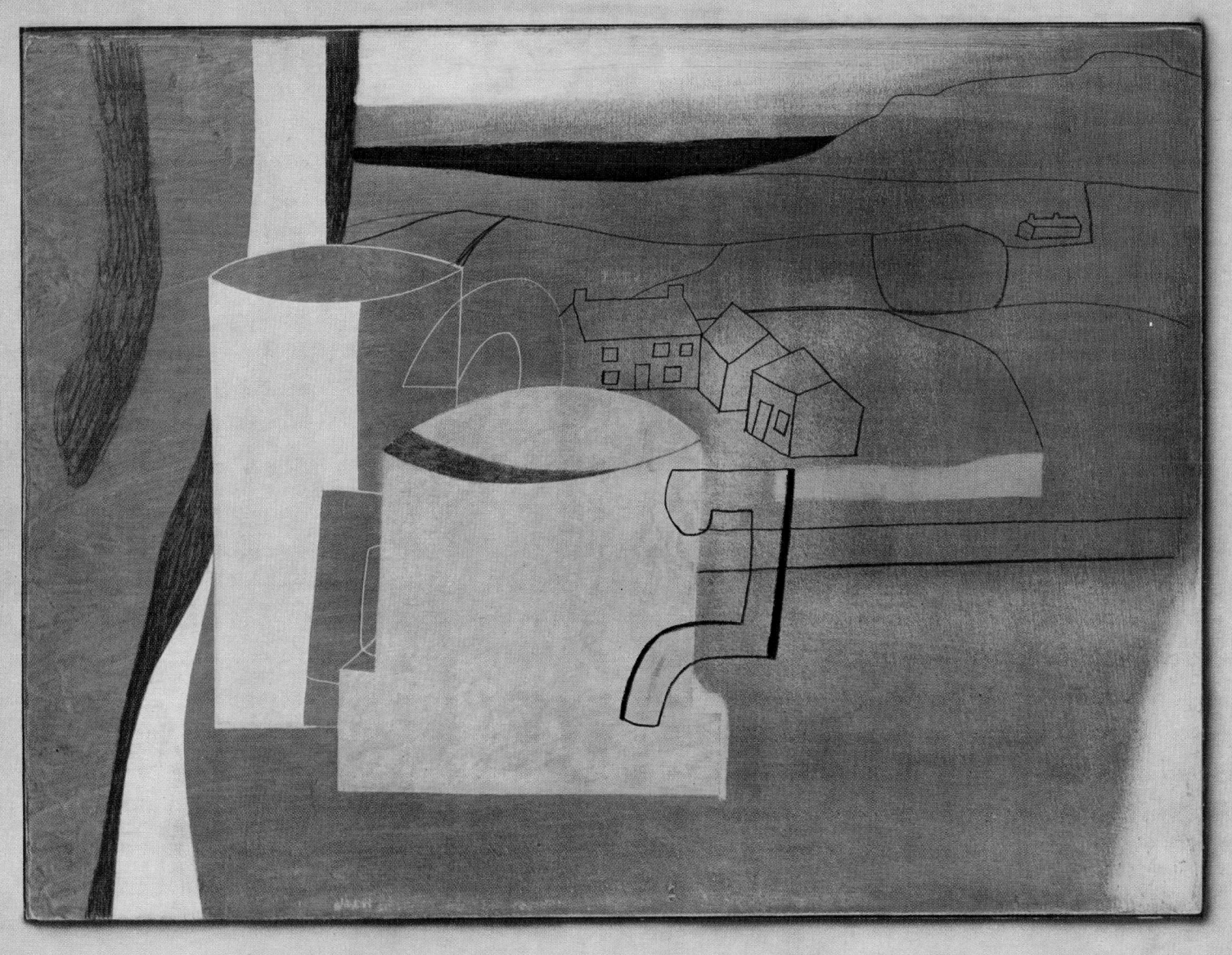

86 *still life and landscape (Towednack) 1943*   *private collection, London*

87 *painting* (milk and plain chocolate) *1933*   collection C. S. Reddihough

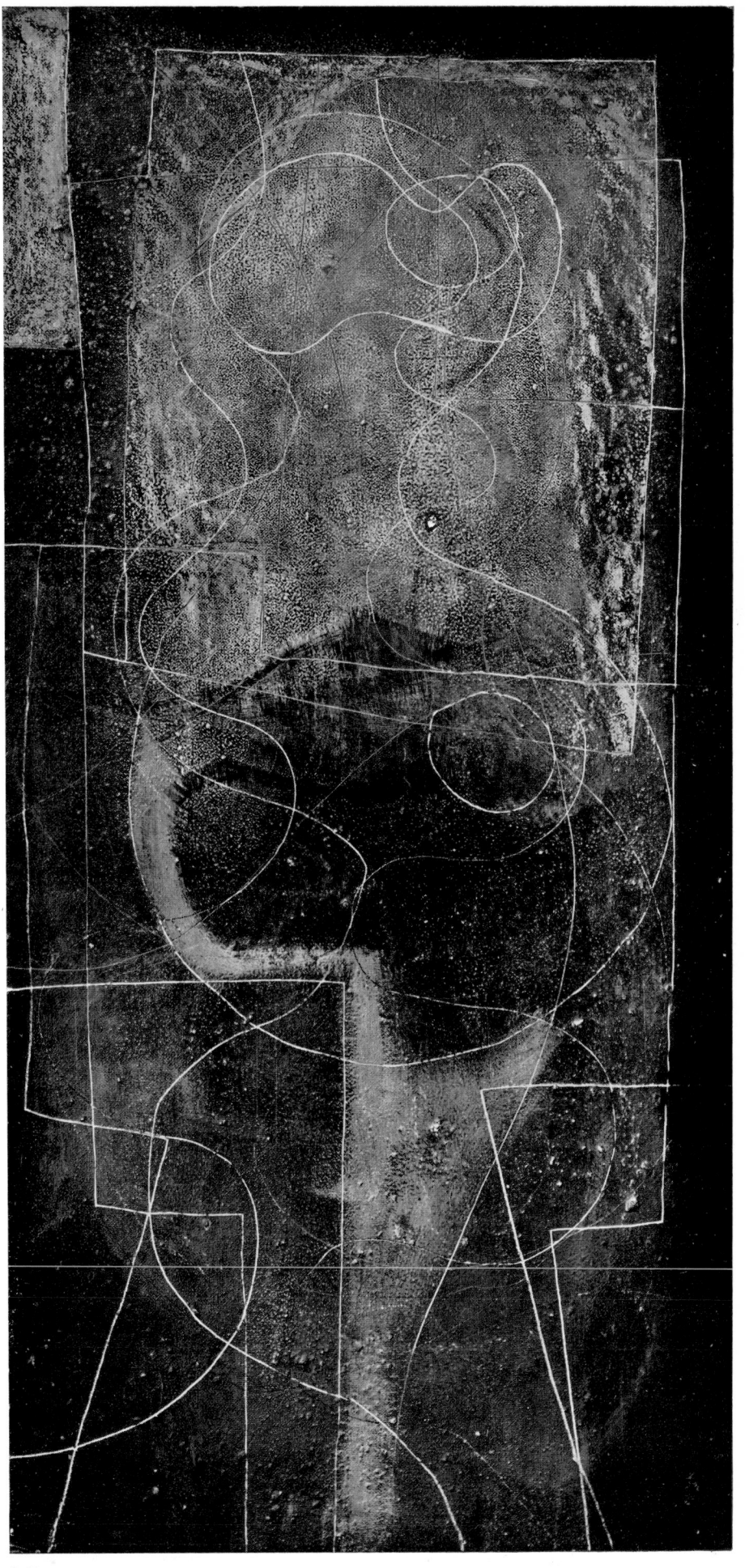

88 *painting 1933*   collection Swindon Art Gallery

89 *painted relief 1935* collection A. J. F. Morton

90 *painting 1935*   collection Winifred Nicholson

91 *white relief 1935*

92 *white relief 1936*

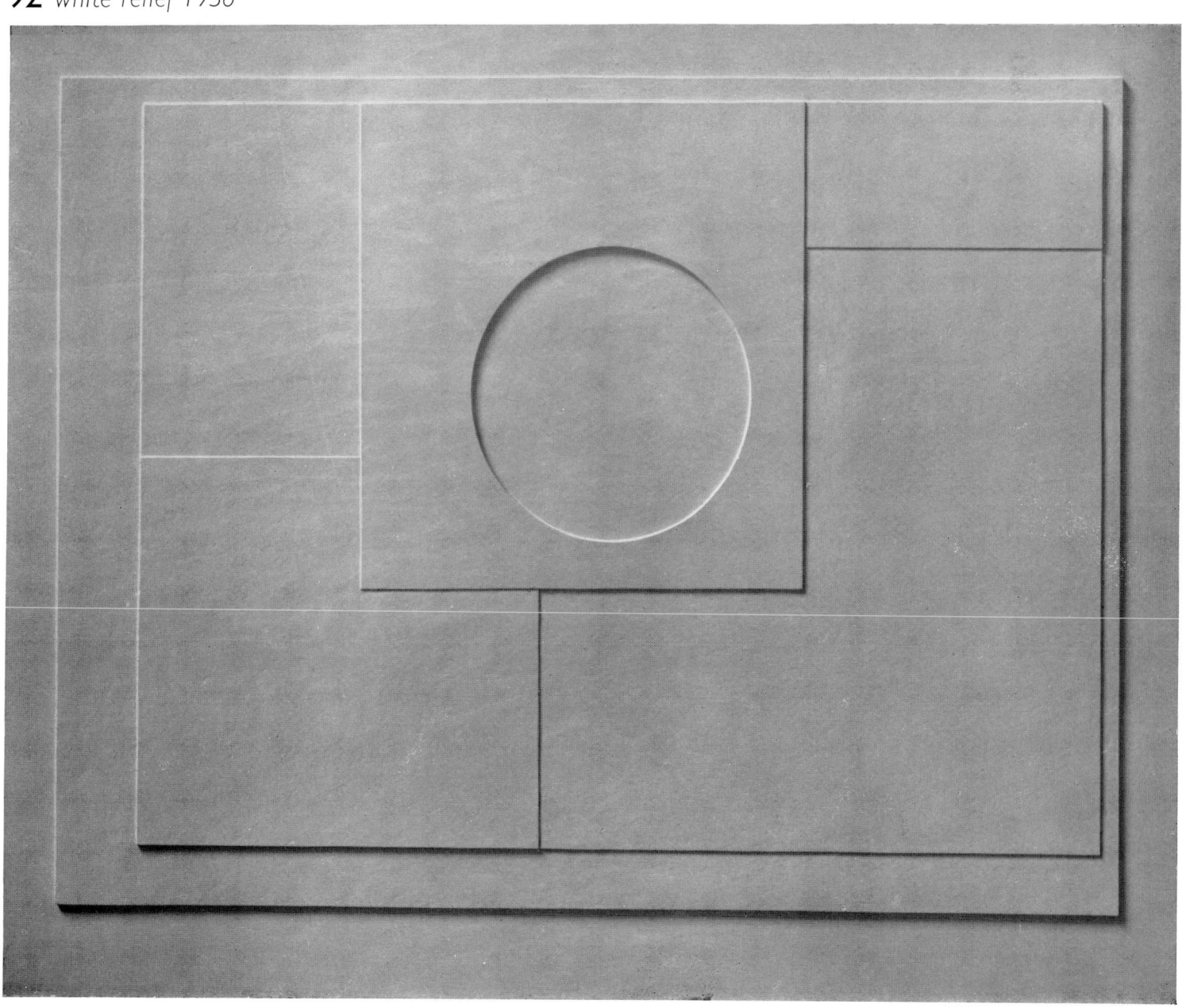

93 *still life 1933–35*   collection Whitney Straight

94 *still life* (Punch and Judy show) *1932–37*   private collection, Brussels Belgium

95 *still life* (Greek landscape) *1931–36*   collection The British Council

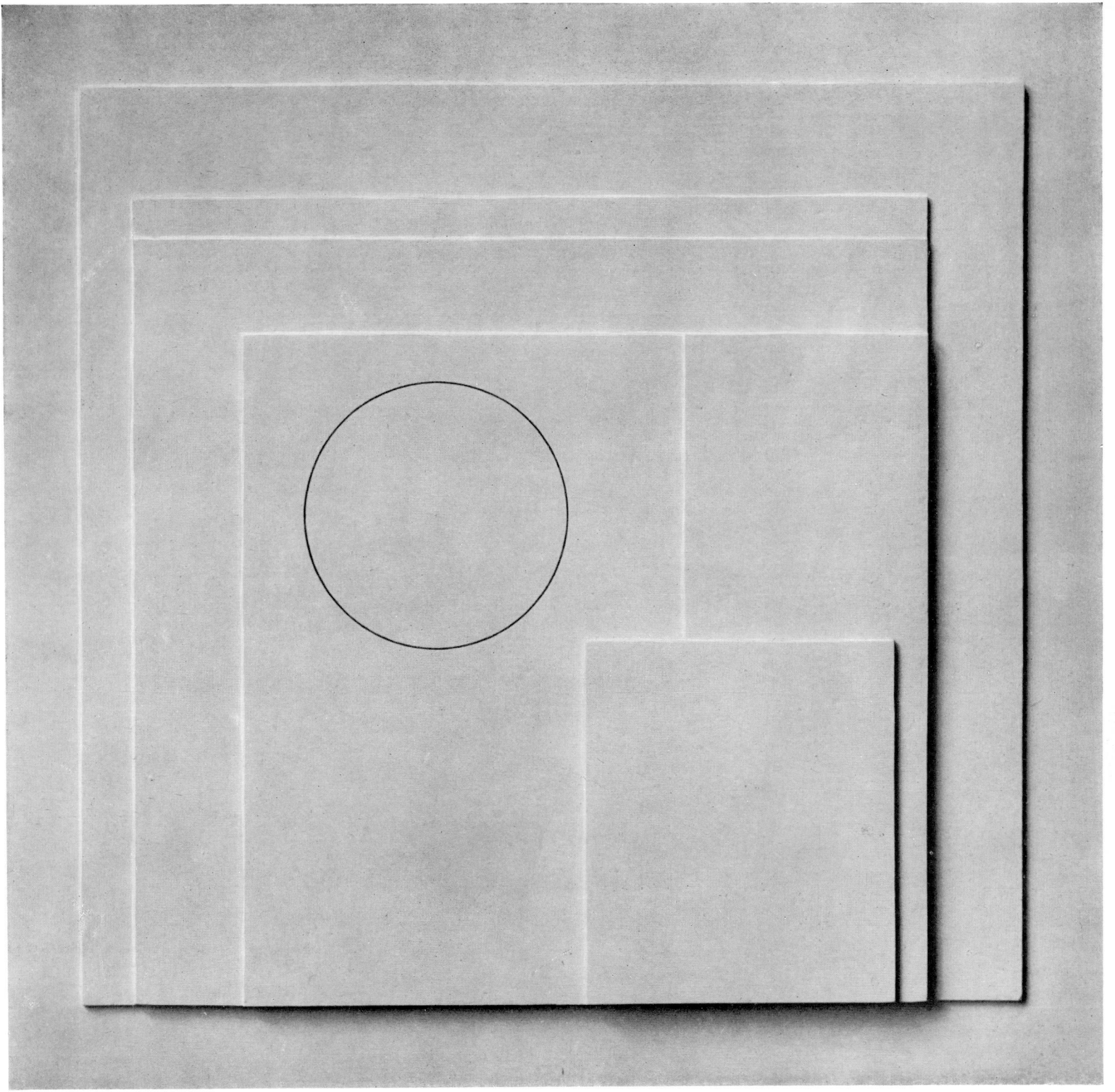

96 *white relief 1939*   collection Winifred Nicholson

version 1   collection Gay Kaye (illustrated)
project   collection Barbara Hepworth
version 2   collection John Wells

97 *painted relief 1941*

98 *white relief 1939* version I collection Peggy Guggenheim *(illustrated)*
project collection Peter Watson
version 2 collection Barbara Hepworth

99 *white relief 1938*   *private collection U.S.A.*

100 *painted relief 1939*   collection Margaret Gardiner

101 *Halse Town 1939–41*   collection E. Q. and Christopher Nicholson

102 *Halse Town c. 1941*

103 *St. Ives rooftops 1940* (version 2)   collection Nancy Roberts

collection Margaret Gardiner

104 *still life 1932–40*

105 *white relief 1938*   collection Adrian Stokes

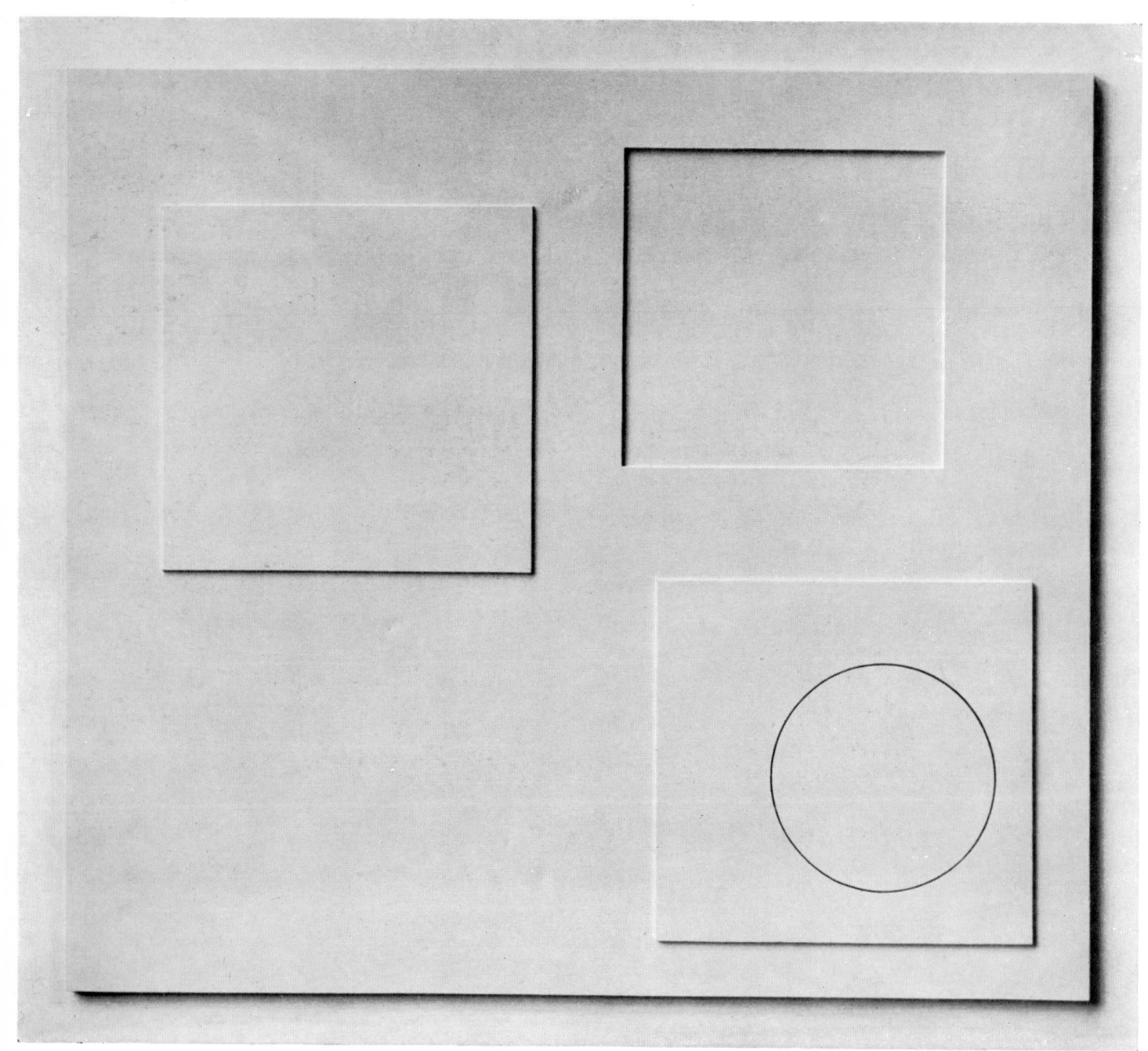

106 *two forms 1940–42*

version 1	collection C. S. Reddihough
project	collection S. and J. L. Martin
version 2	collection R. F. F. Allen
version 3	collection Federick Seacrest (U.S.A.)
version 4 (midget)	collection Peter Watson
version 5 (midget)	collection Graham Sutherland
version 6 (midget)	collection L. Harvey
version 7 (midget)	collection the late Curt Valentin (U.S.A.)
version 8 (midget)	(illustrated)

107 *painting 1943*

version 1 (illustrated)   Munson Williams, Proctor Institute, Utica, New York
project   collection M. Ricardo Pearce
version 2 (midget)   collection Winifred Nicholson
version 3 (midget)   collection Margot Eates
version 4 (midget)   collection S. and J. L. Martin
version 5 (midget)   collection Gladys Whiting
version 6 (midget)   collection Fello Atkinson
version 7

108 *drawing 1936*   version 1   collection Suzy and George L. K. Morris (illustrated)
version 2   collection E. H. Ramsden

collection Peter Watson

Halse Town 1939

109

collection J. R. M. Brumwell

110 *painting 1937*

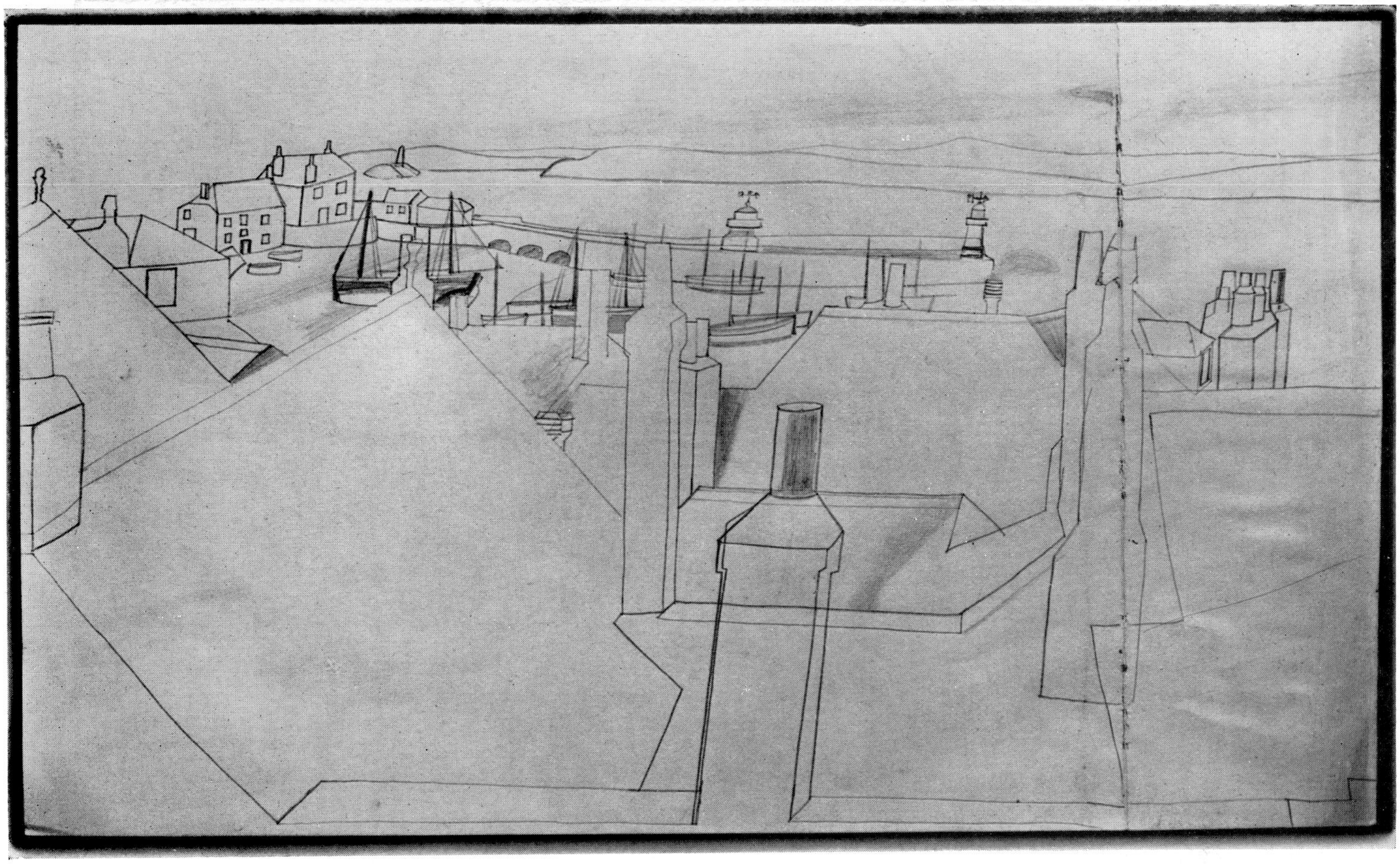

111 *St. Ives rooftops 1940*

112 *still life 1945*   collection John Summerson

113 *St. Ives 1940*   collection C. S. Reddihough

114 *painted relief 1940*   version 1   collection Nicolete Gray (illustrated)
version 2   collection Arman Bartelos, U.S.A.

115 *still life 1930–42*   collection S and J. L. Martin

116 *painted relief 1941*   (version 1)   collection C. S. Reddihough

117 *white relief 1936*   collection N. Gabo

118 *painted relief 1939*   version 1   collection Museum of Modern Art, New York (*illustrated*)
version 2   collection A. J. F. Morton

collection Elsie Myers

119 *Higher Carnstabba farm 1944*

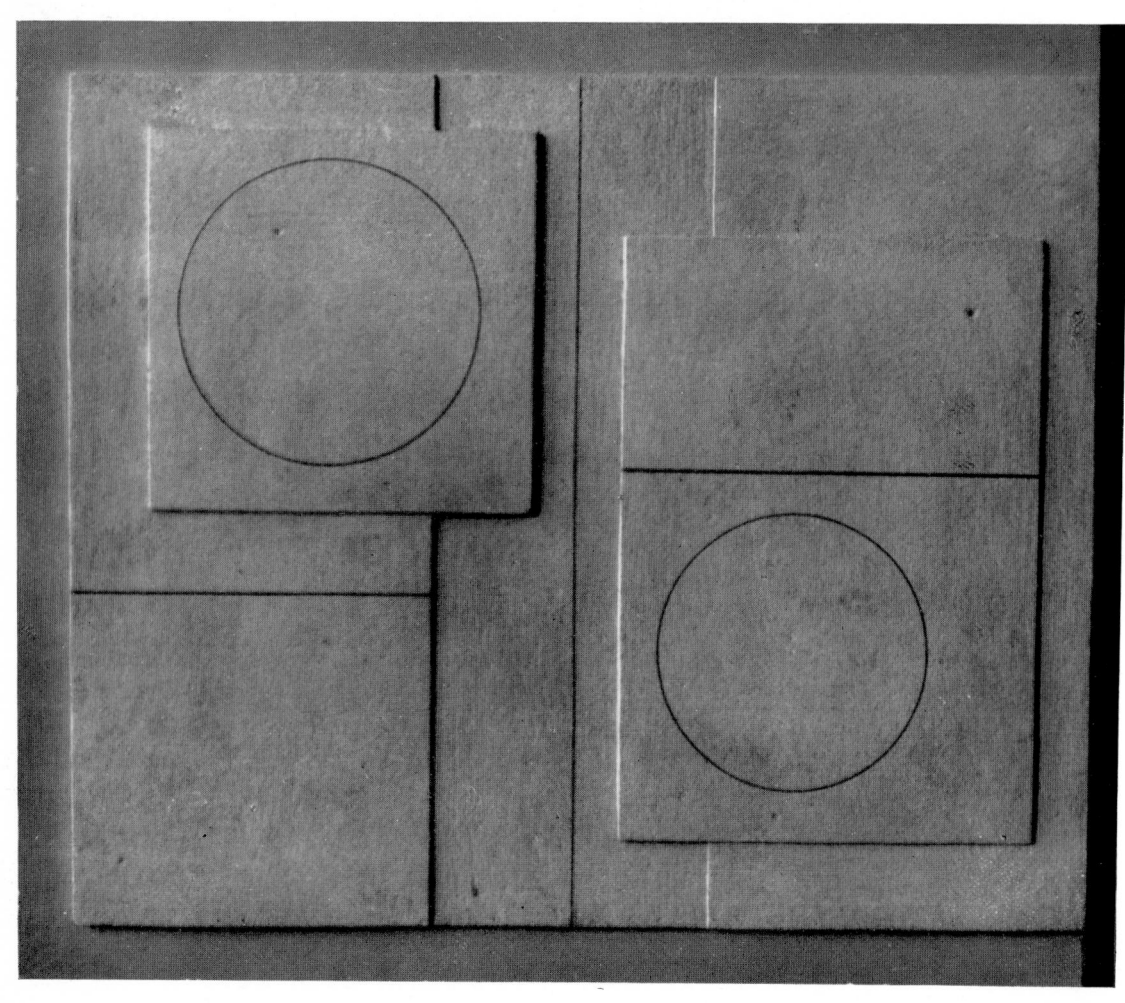

collection S. and J. L. Martin

120 *relief 1944*

collection Helen Sutherland

playing cards 1945

121

collection F. L. S. Murray

122 *still life* (Chinese) *1945*

123 *painted relief 1943–44*

version 1   collection Ian Gibson Smith (illustrated)
project   collection Barbara Hepworth
version 2   collection M. J. Tambimuttu

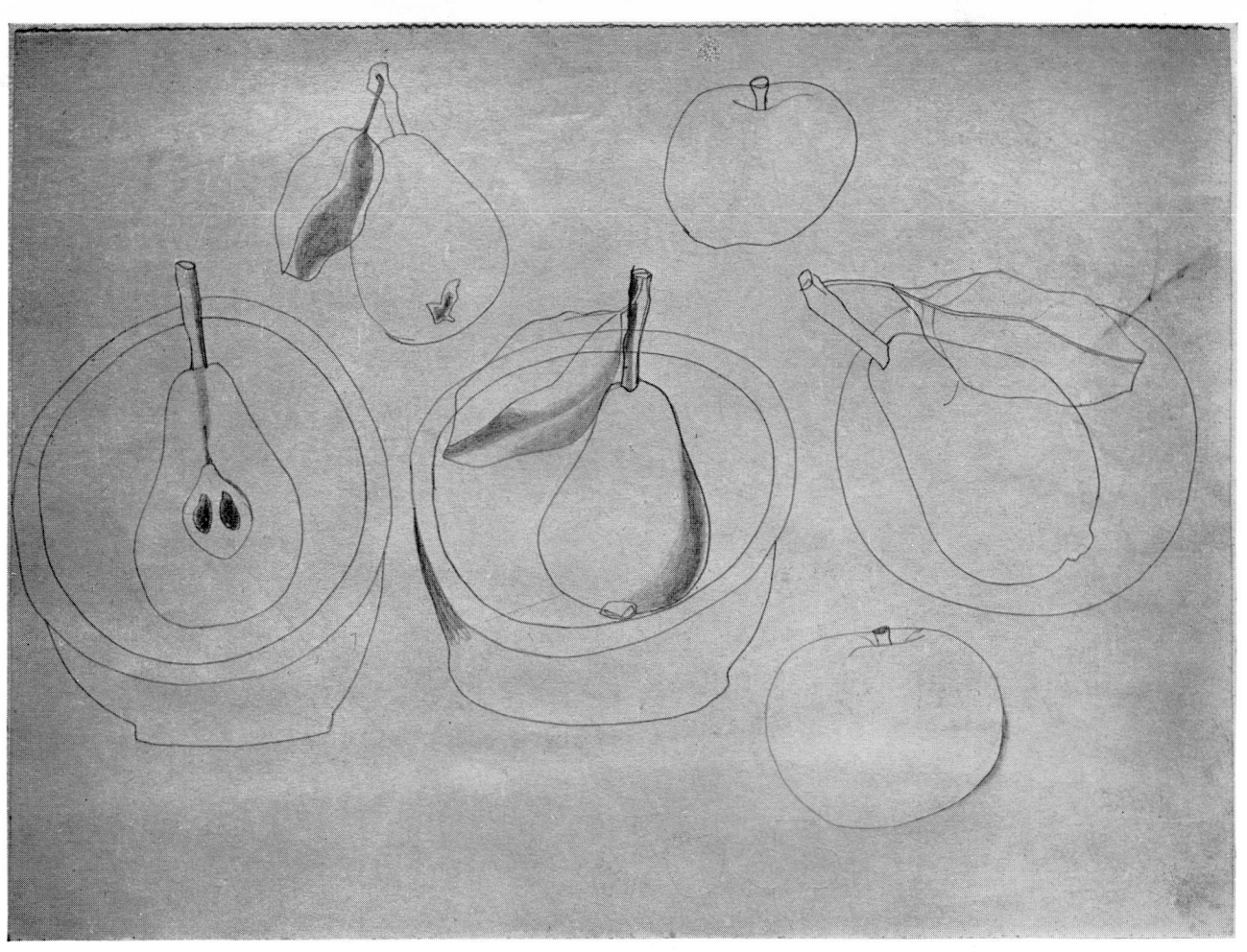

124 *fruit 1944*   collection J. P. Ducrest (France

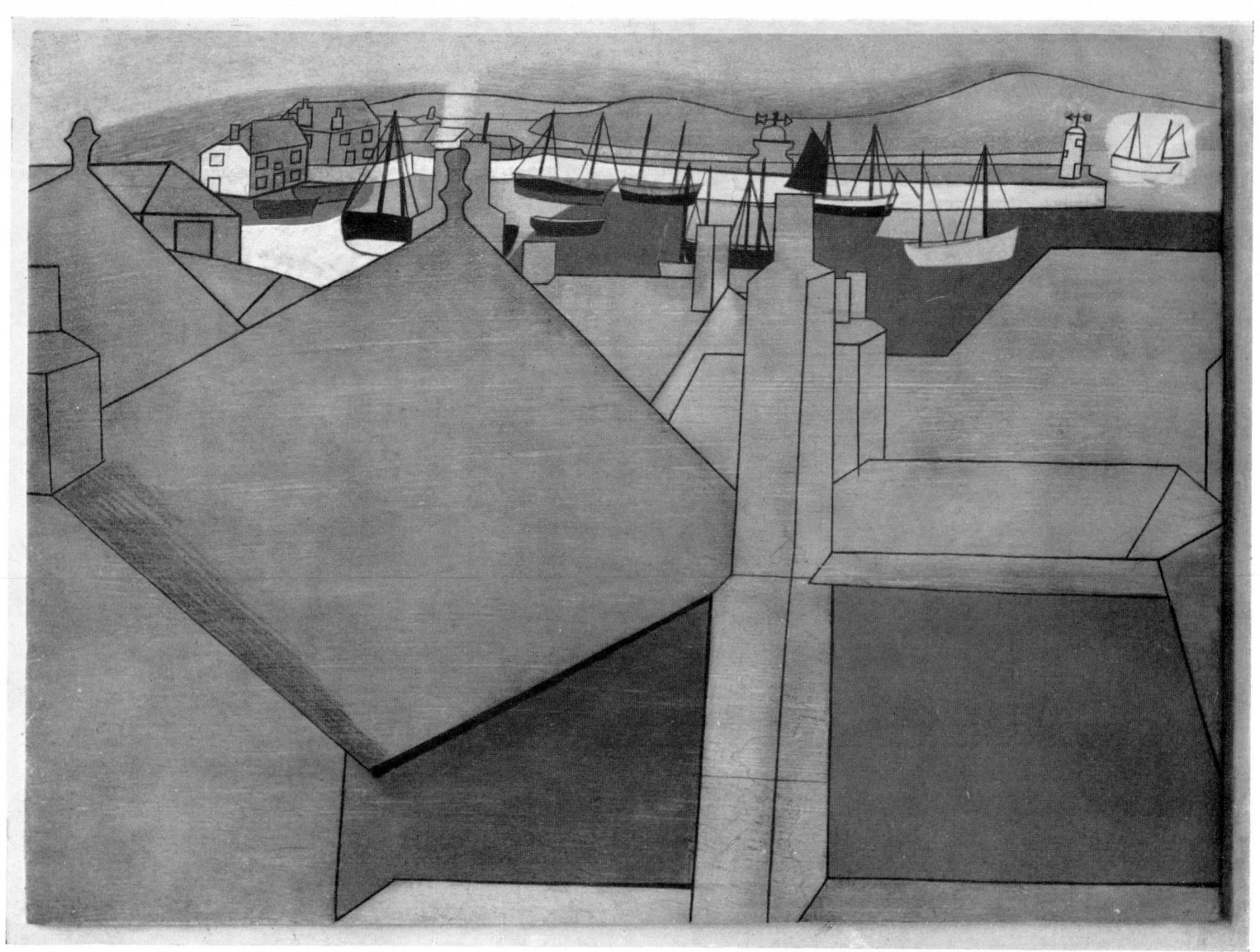

125 *St. Ives rooftops 1940* (version 1)   collection Helen Sutherland

126 *Cornish landscape* (Lelant) *c. 1940–41*

127 project 1941 *collection Ann Archdale*

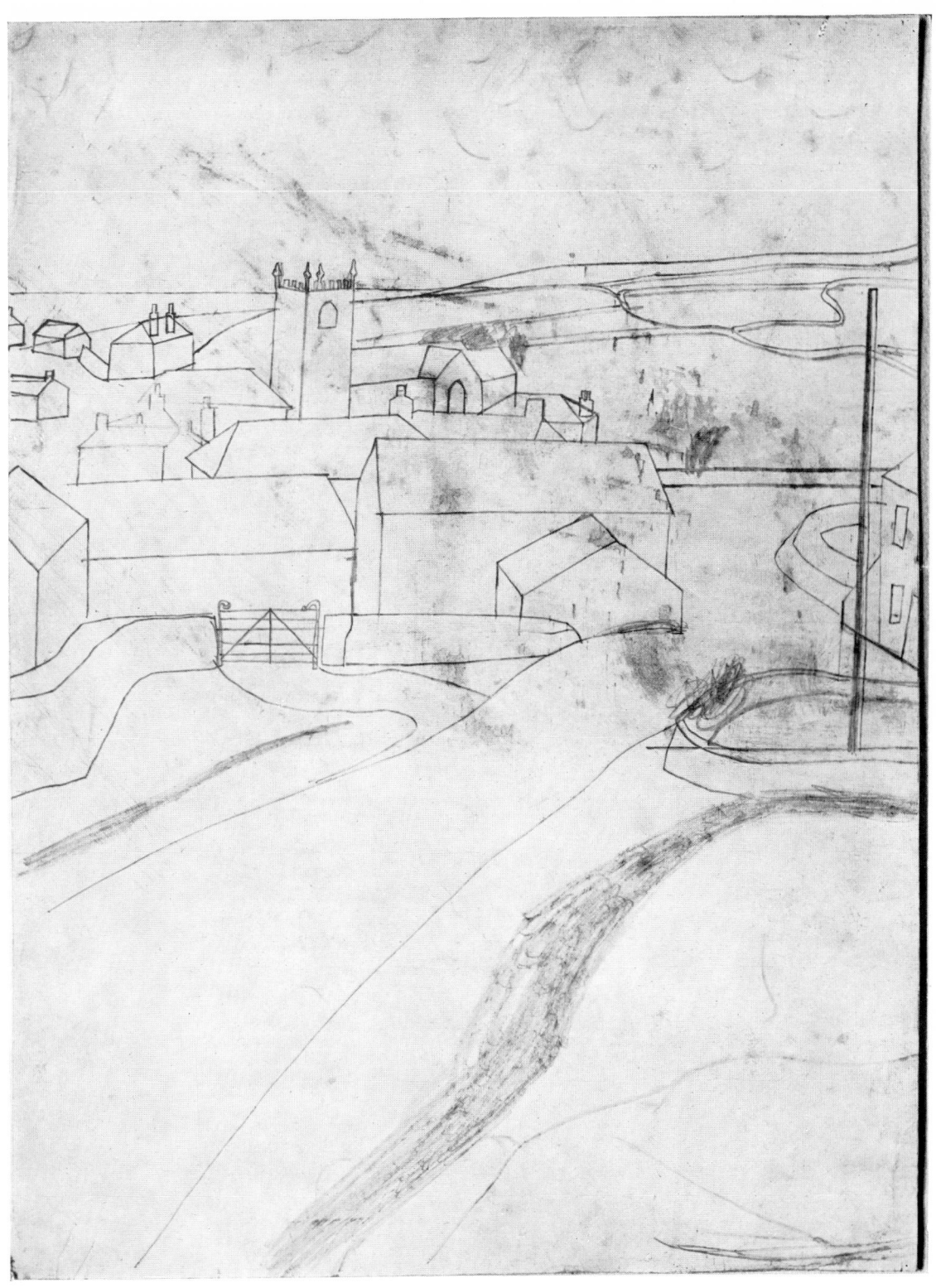

128 *Zennor, 1941* collection Contemporary Art Society

129 *painted relief 1941*

version 1   collection S. and J. L. Martin (illustrated)
project   collection Herbert Read
version 2   collection G. L. K. Morris (painting)
version 3   collection John Wells (painting)
version 4   collection G. Hammond Steel (painting)
version 5   collection H. S. Ede (painting)

30 *white relief 1938*   *version I (illustrated)*   *project collection Pat Davies*

collection I. P. Turner

Mousehole, summer—47

131

collection Tate Gallery

132 *St. Ives 1943—45*

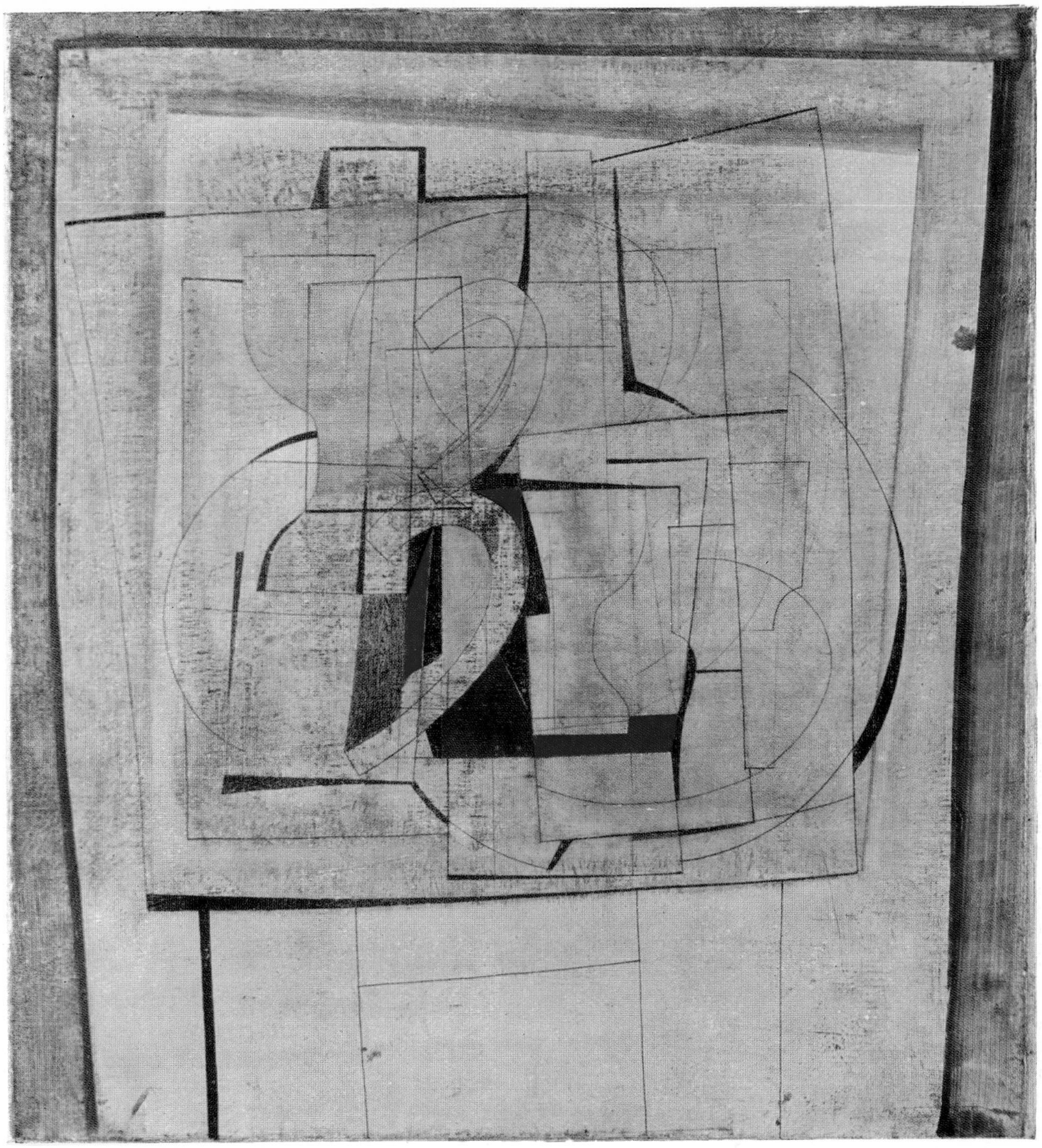

133 *still life 1945*

134 *playing cards 1945*

135 *parrot's eye 1945*   *collection Barbara Hepworth*

136 *three mugs 1944*

137 *project 1942*

collection E. Q. and Christopher Nicholson

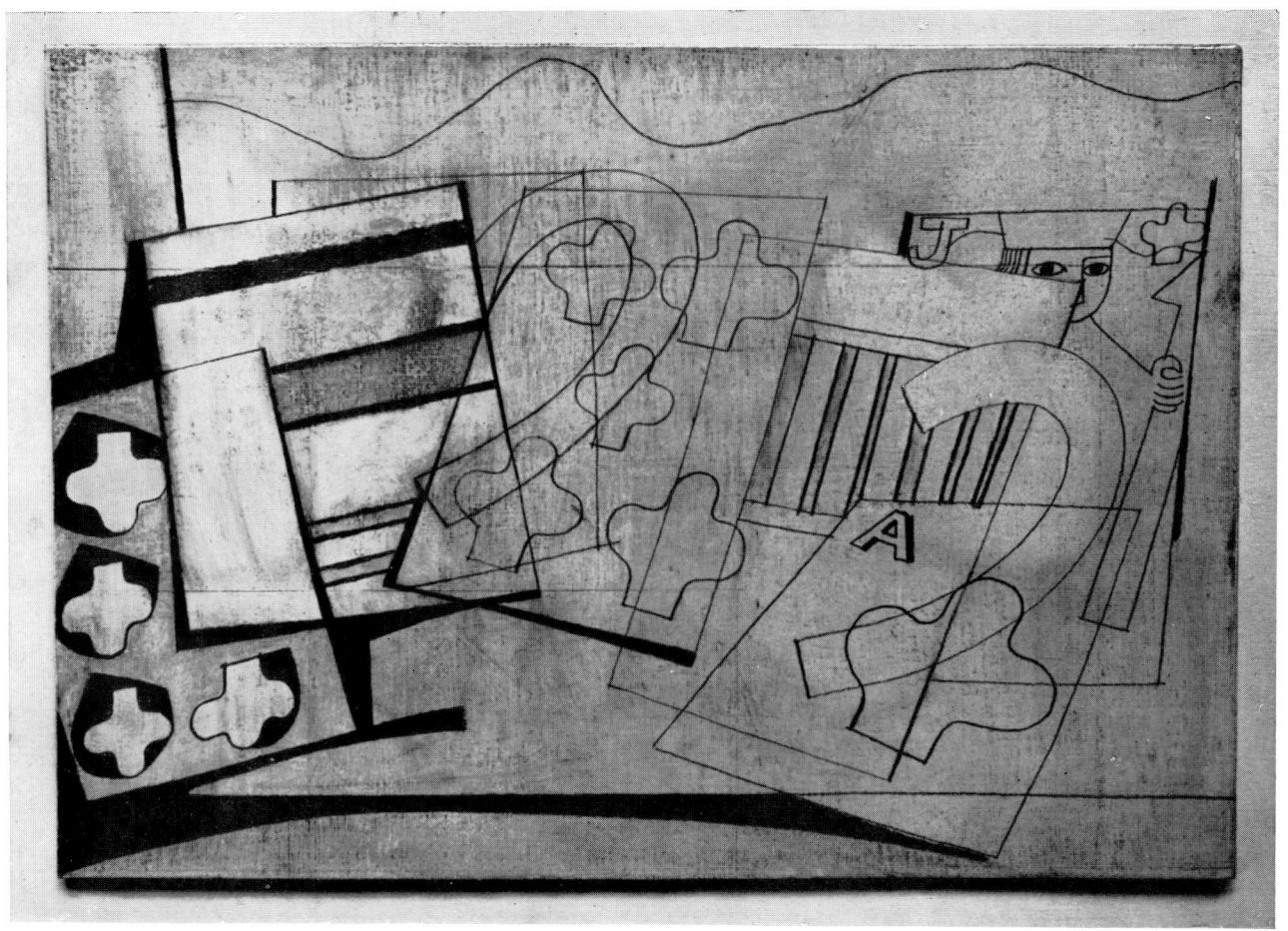

138 *playing cards 1945*

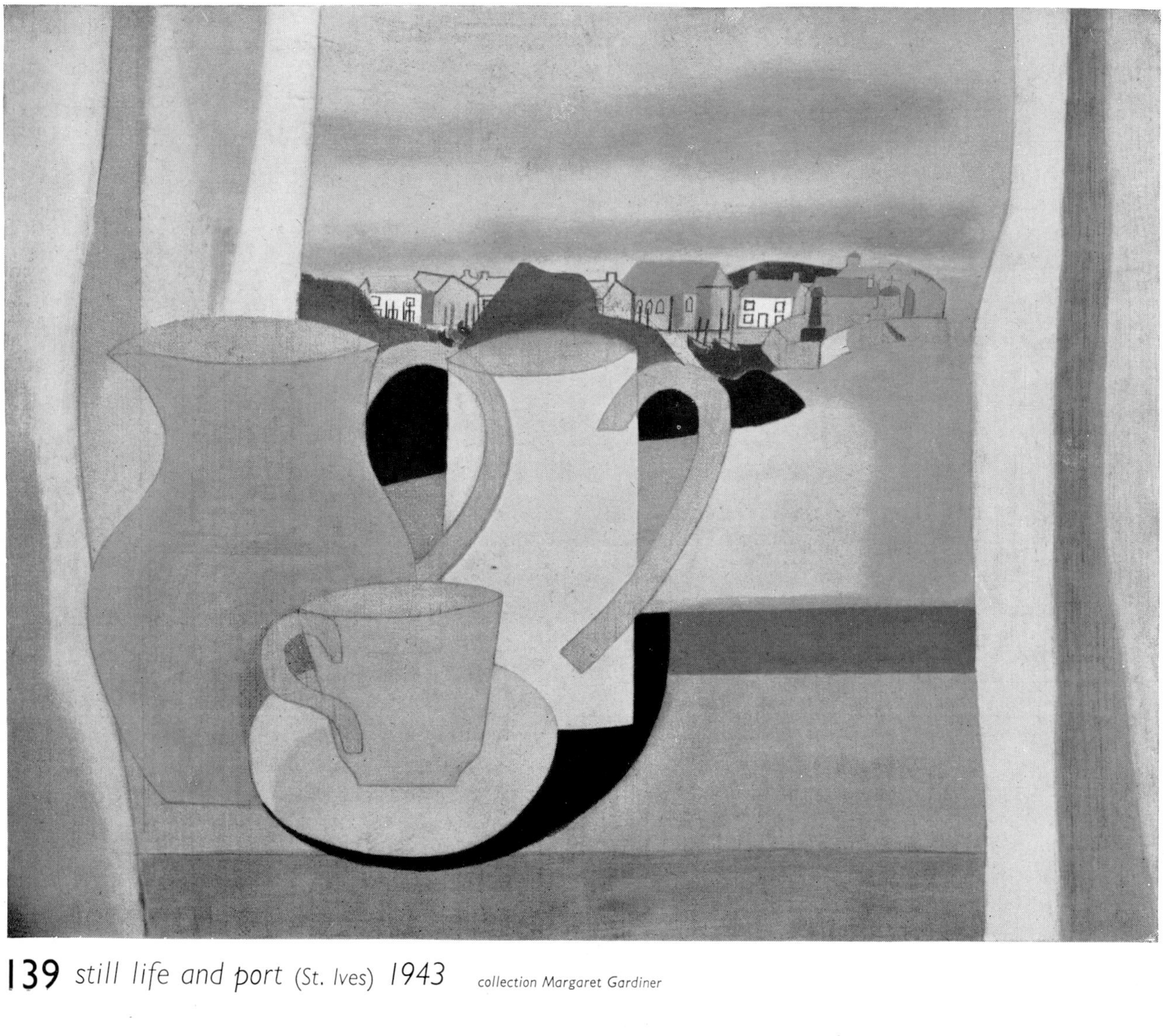

139 *still life and port* (St. Ives) *1943* collection Margaret Gardiner

140 *still life* (Mount's Bay) July 20–47

141 *still life* 1945   collection D. Rosner

142 *painting 1943–44*   collection Kent Bragaline Inc.

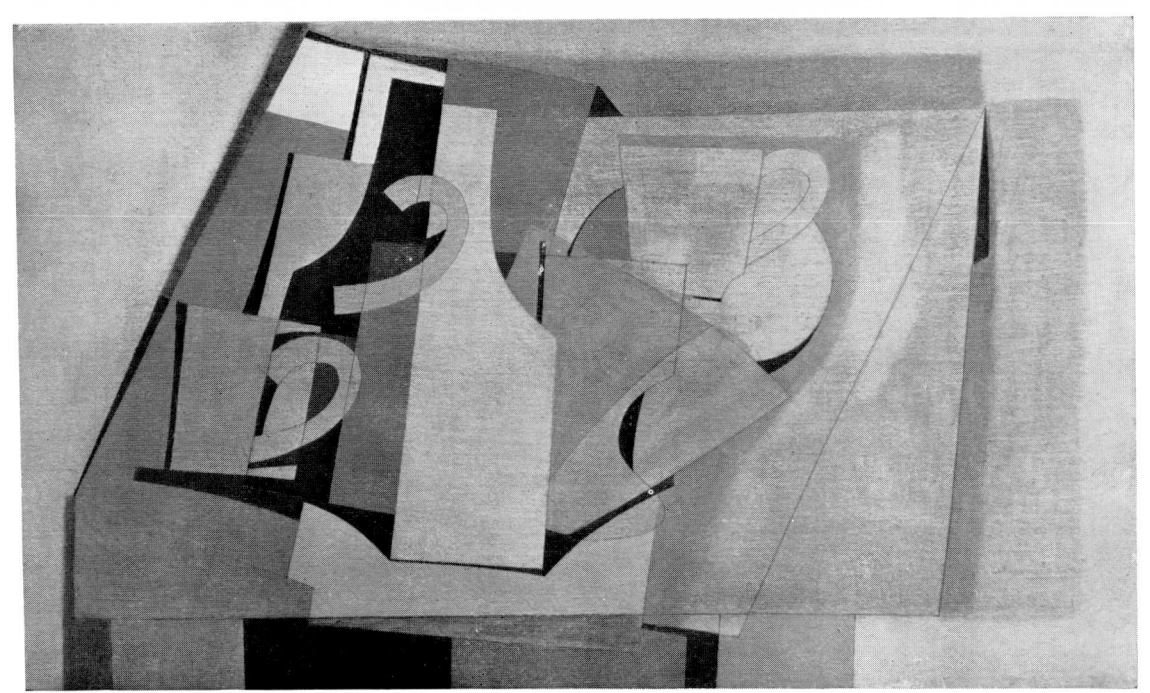

143 *still life 1945* collection S. and J. L. Martin

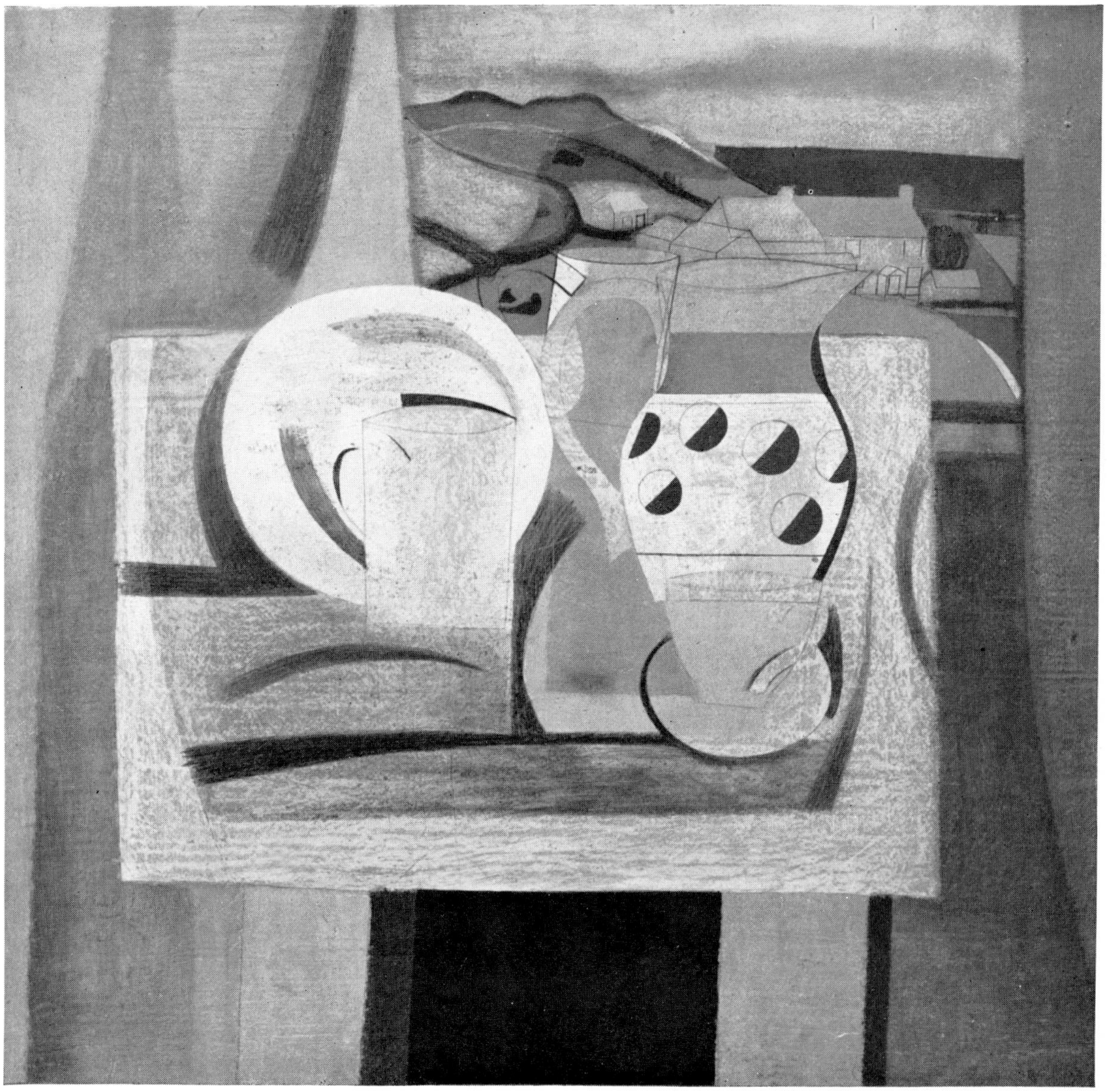

collection International Business Machines Corporation, New York

still life and Cornish landscape 1944

144

collection Dorothy Morland
145 *still life* (Fra Angelico) *1946*

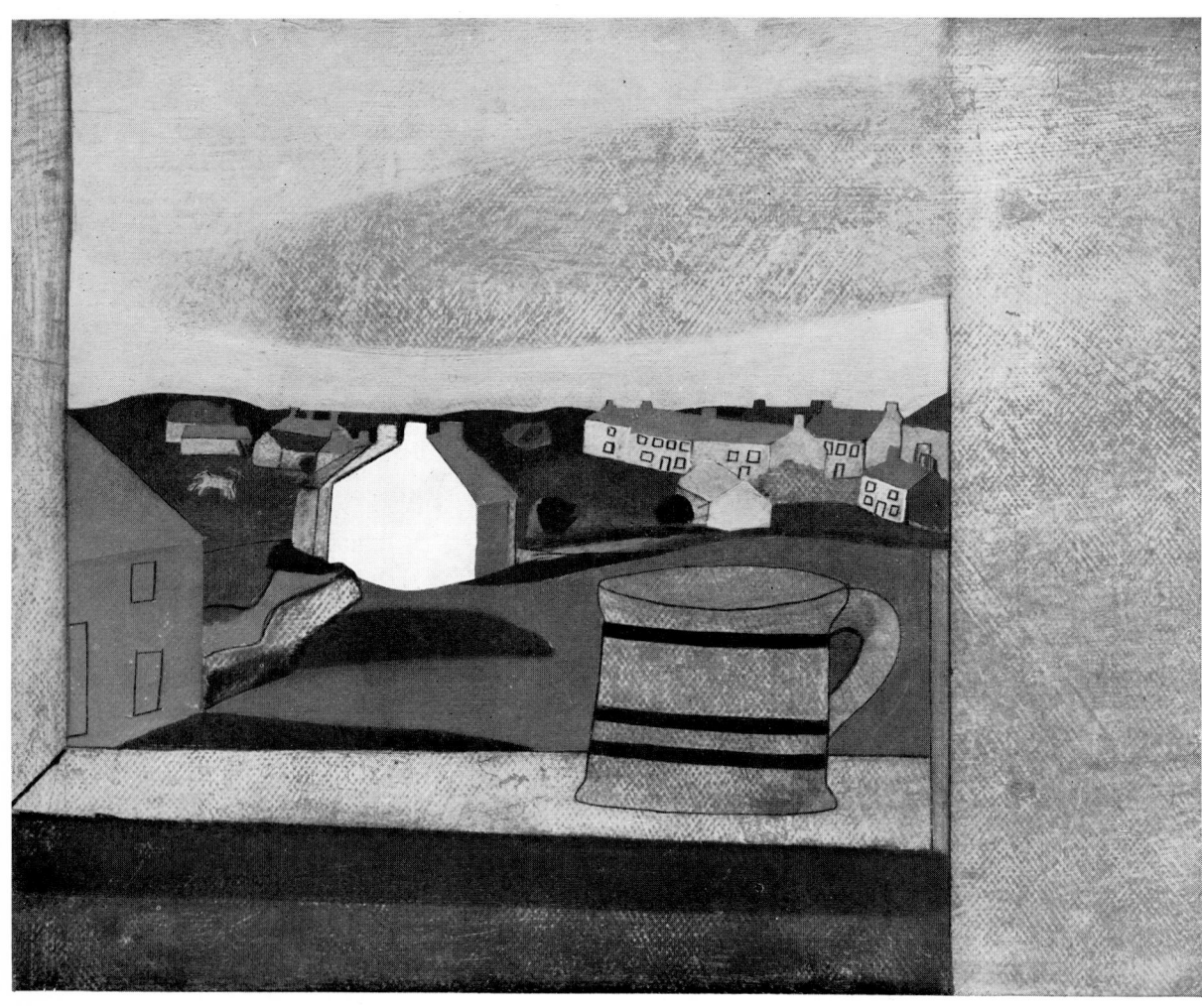

collection Mortimer Bennitt
146 *Halse Town 1942*

collection James Archdale

147 *painted relief* (*Arabian desert*) *1944–45*

version 1   collection Michael Ventris
version 2   collection Margaret Gardiner (illustrated)
version 3   collection S. and J. L. Martin
version 4   collection Frederick Gibberd
version 5   collection F. L. S. Murray

148 *painted relief 1943*

collection E. C. Gregory
painted relief 1943
149

collection Miller Company, Meriden, Conn. (U.S.A.)
150 *goblets 1947*

private collection Brussels

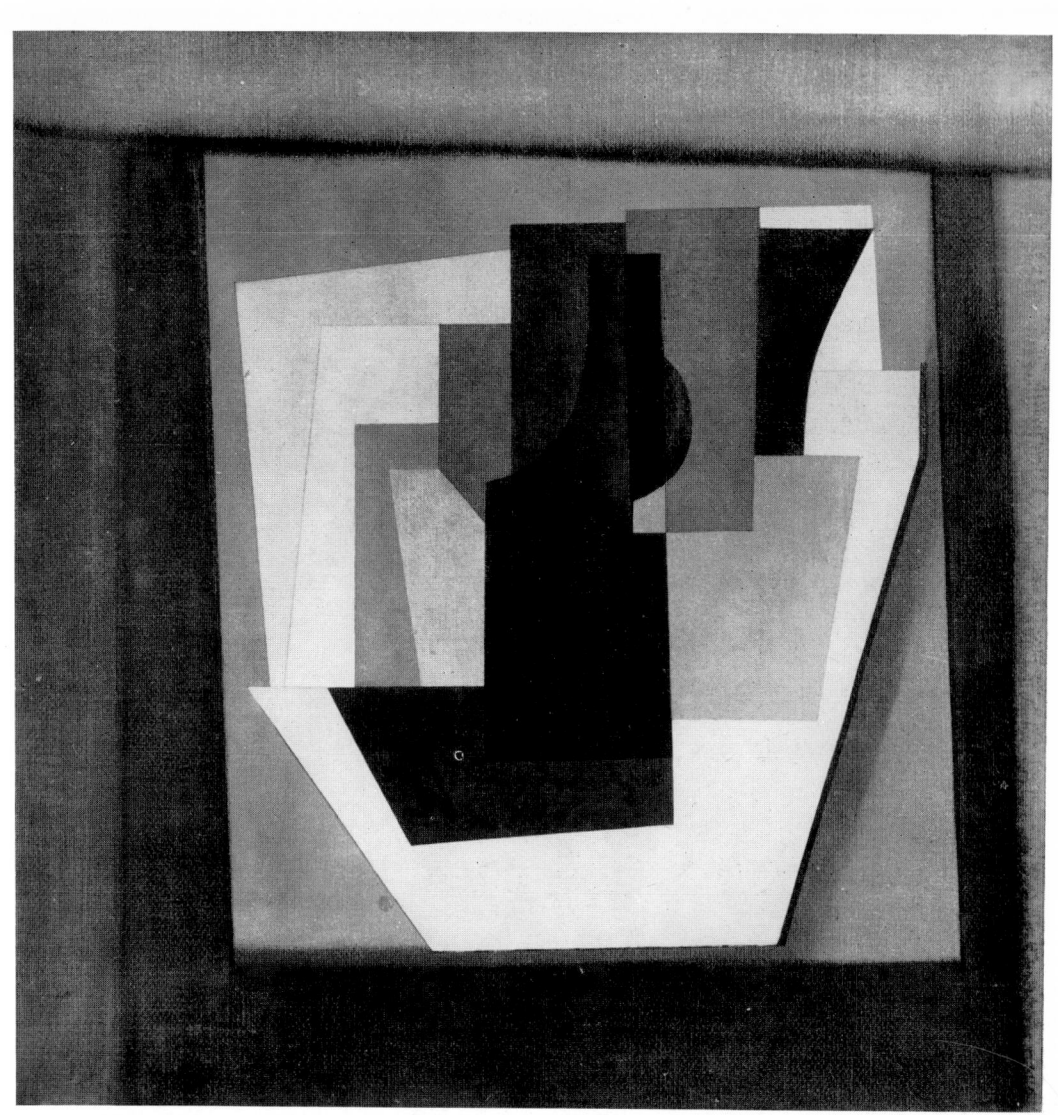

150a *still life* (shop window) *1946*

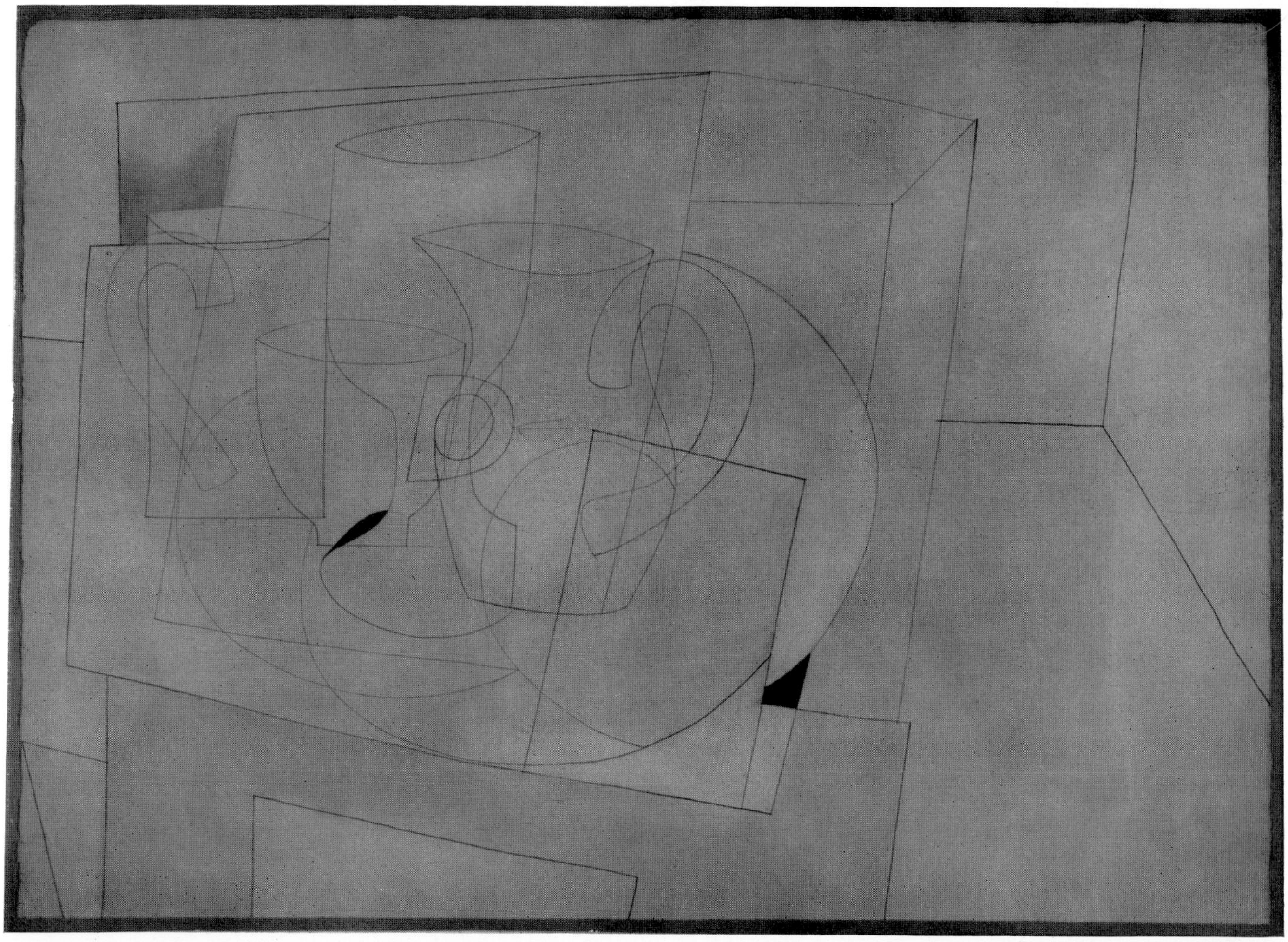

collection The British Council

still life on table

1947

150b

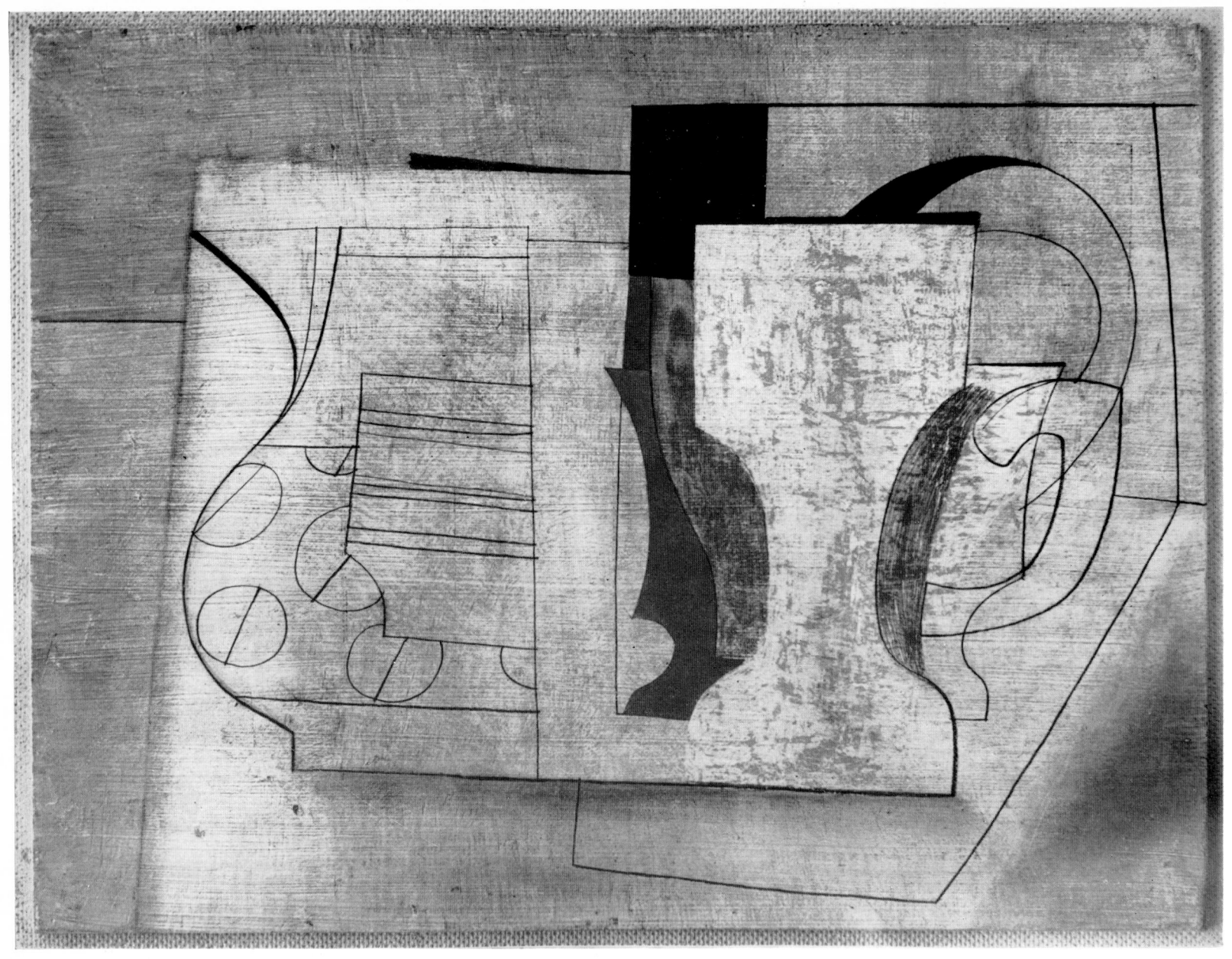

150c *still life June 16–47*   collection F. L. S. Murray

151 *Little Trevarrack 1945*   *collection Edward Sackville-West*

152 *project 1943*

153 *still life 1946*

154 *project 1945*

155 *two mugs 1944*

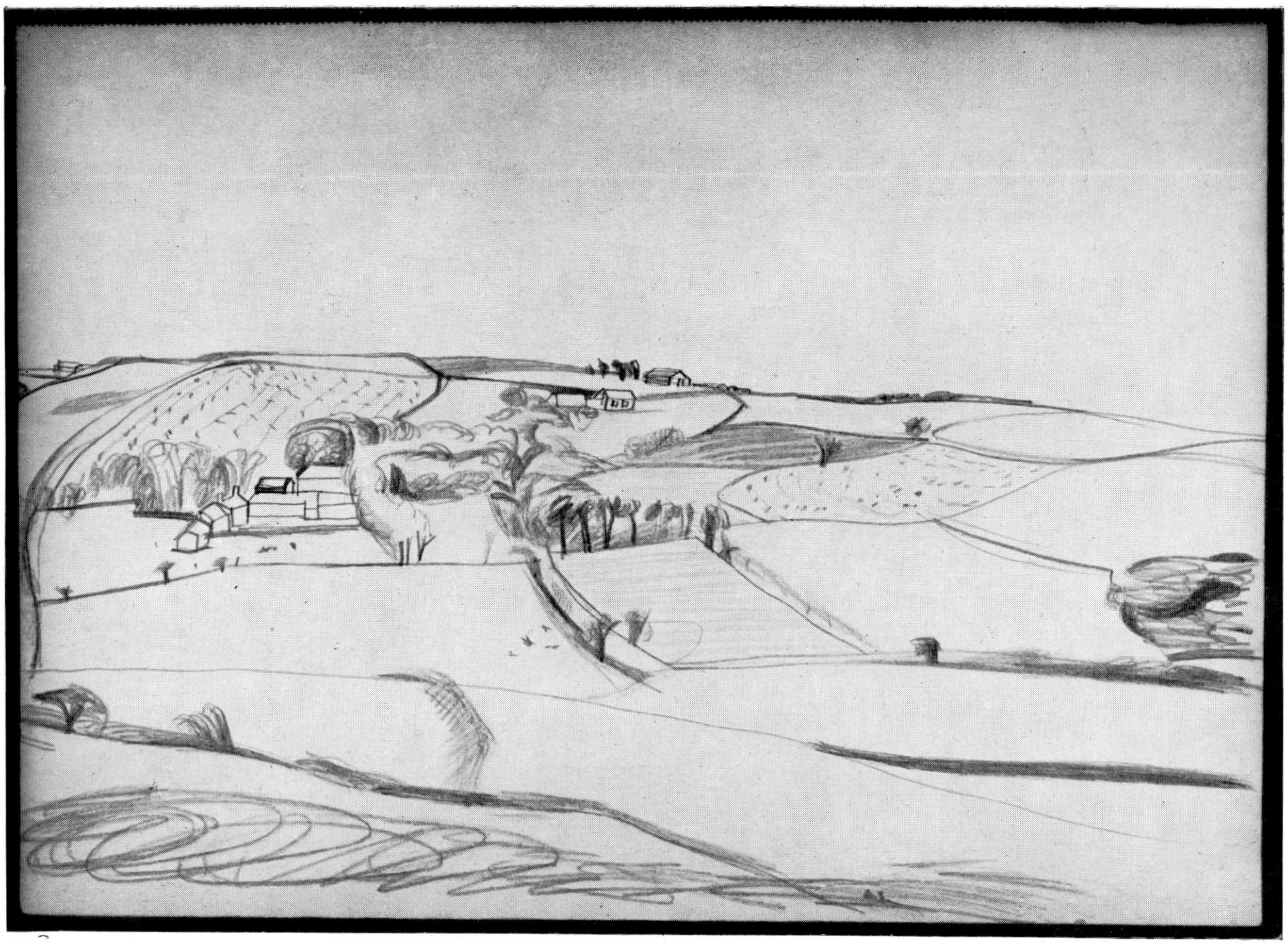

collection Lily Macdonald

Cornish Landscape, summer–45

156

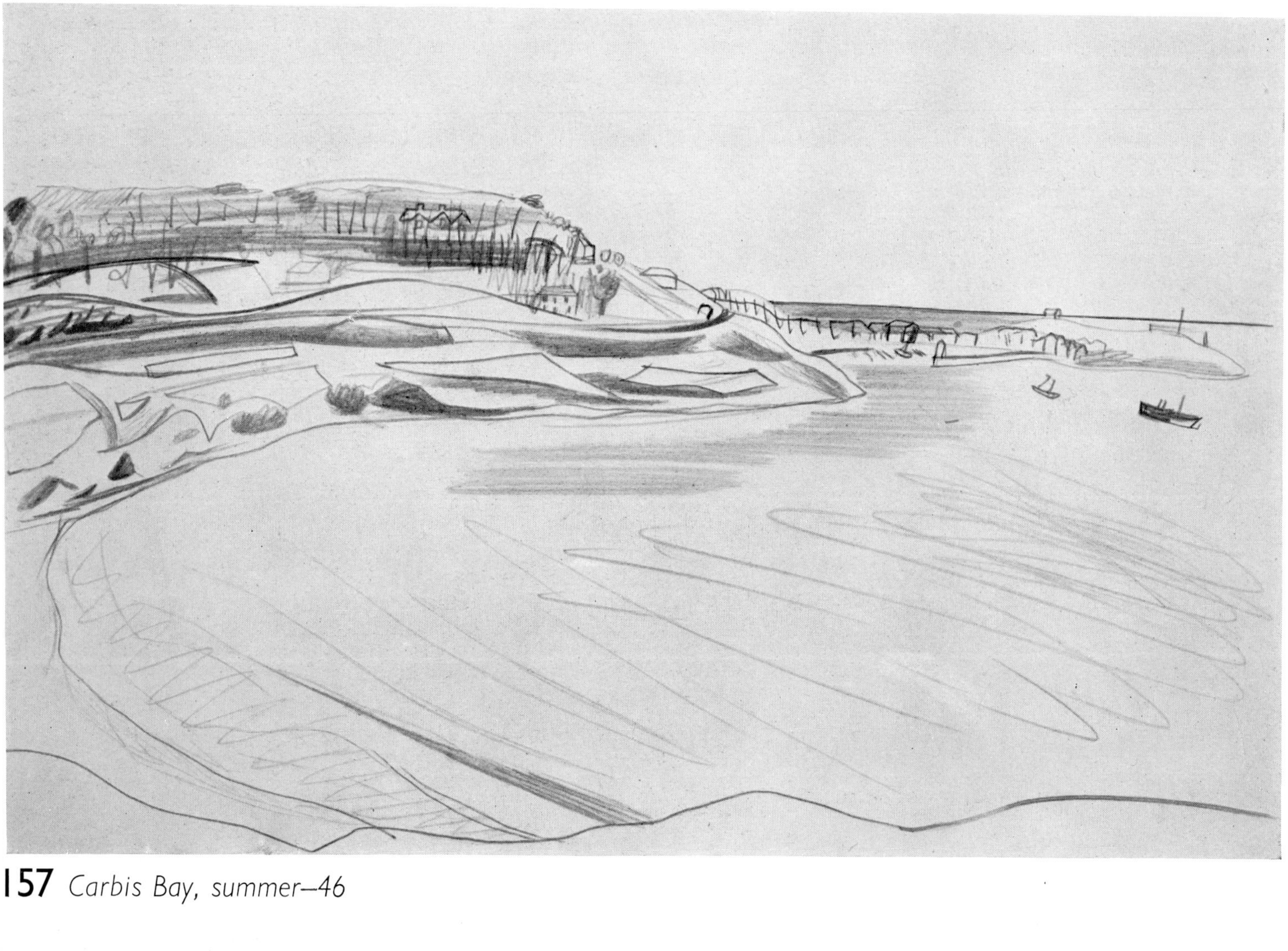

157 *Carbis Bay, summer–46*

158 *still life 1945*   collection Tate Gallery

159 *painting* (yellow on grey) *1946* collection Joseph Brewer (U.S.A.)

160 *St. Ives, 1945*   collection A. J. McN. Reid

collection Kenneth Clark

161 *mug and goblets 1947*

162 *Towednack, summer—46*   collection C. S. Reddihough

163 *still life 1943–44*   collection Lefevre Gallery

64 *painting* (Arizona) *1946*   collection Mainichi Shimbum, Tokyo

165 *May 21—48* (cat not under table)   *collection Jan de Graaf (U.S.A.)*

166 *painted relief 1943*   collection Barbara Hepworth

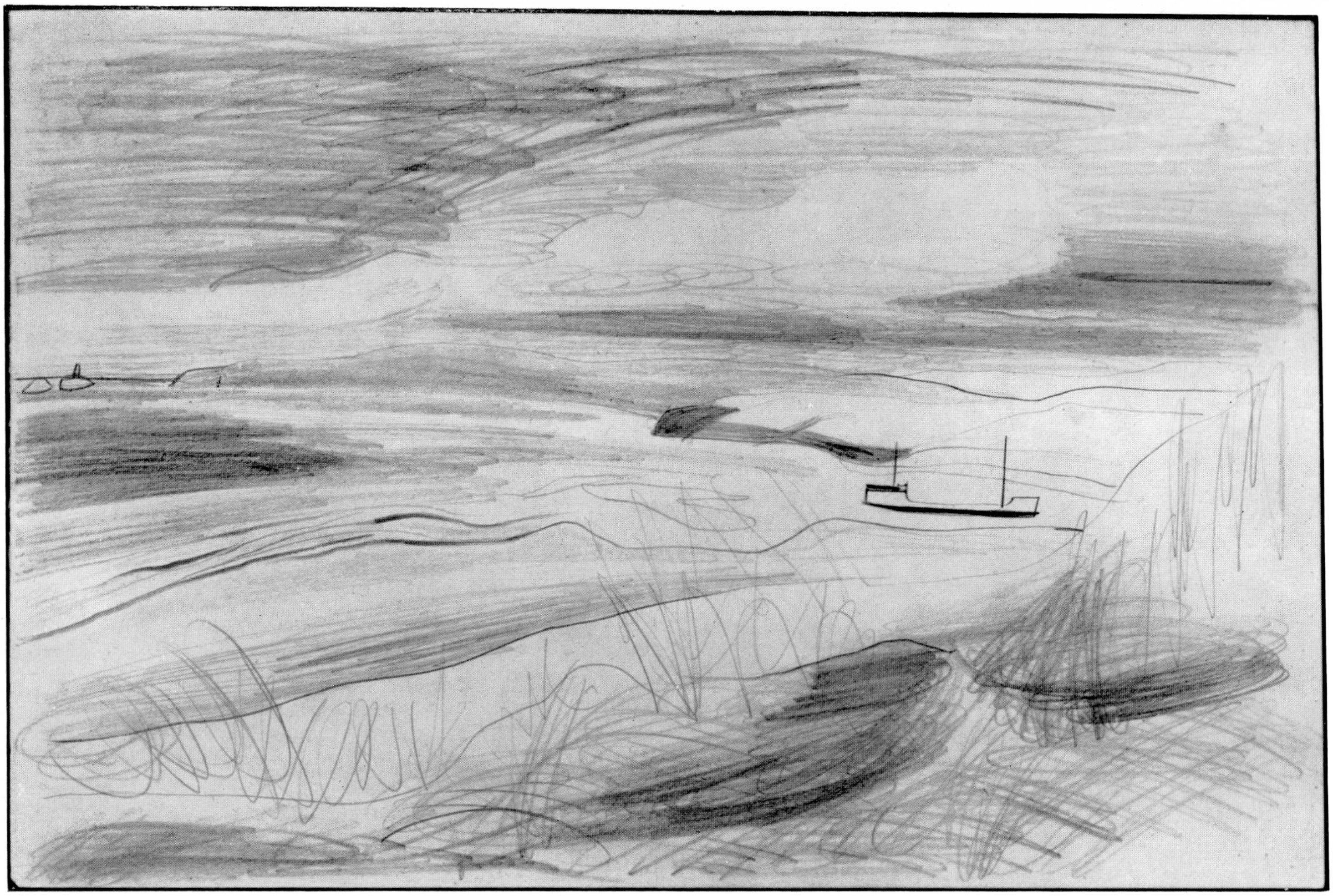

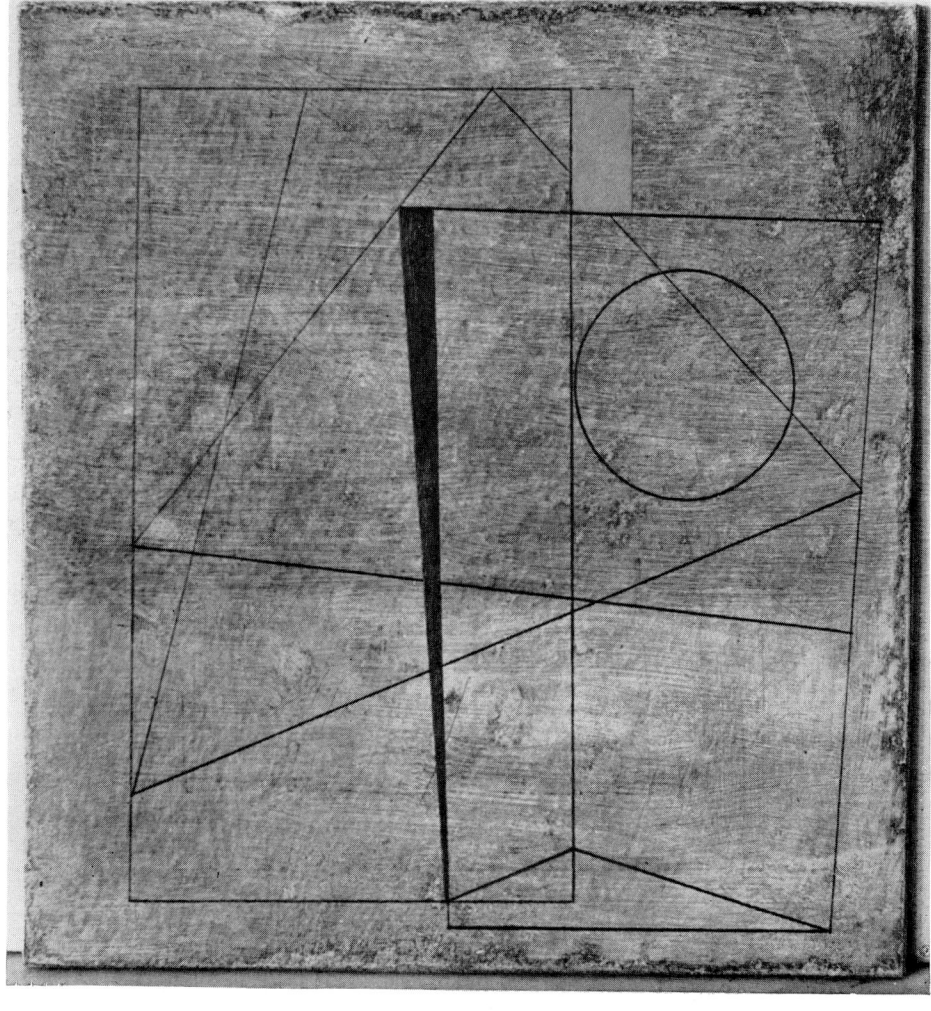

167 *Hayle estuary, May–46*

collection George E. Dix (U.S.A.)

168 *project* (*green-brown*), *February 13–47*

169 *still life* (Zennor Head) *1946*   collection The British Council

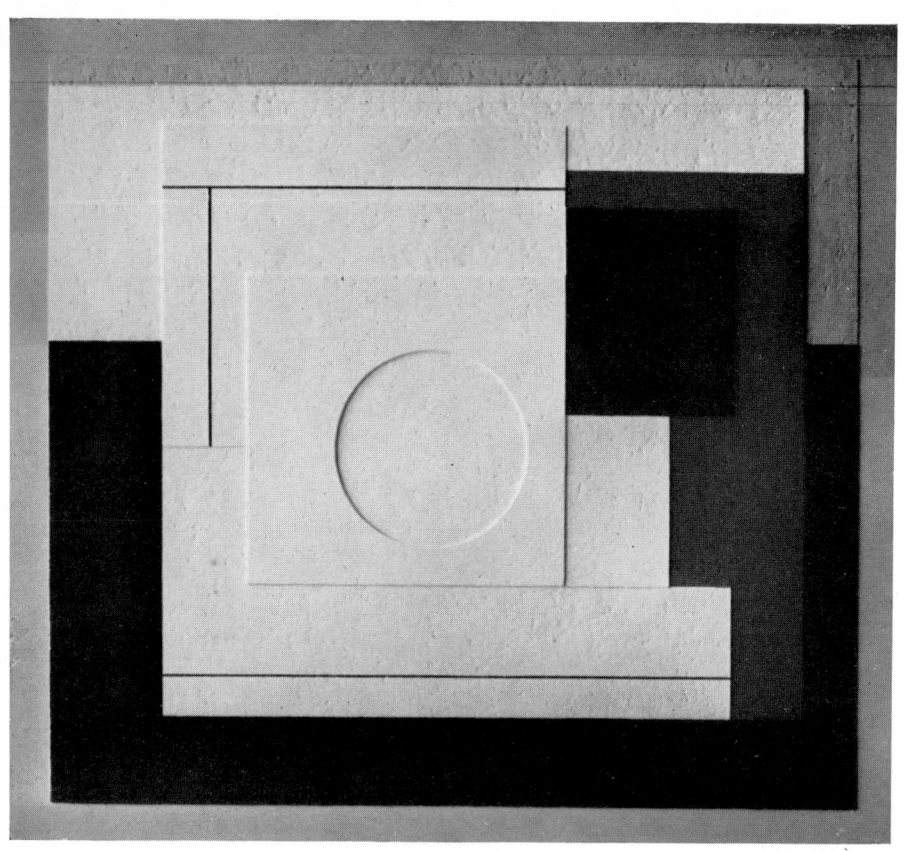

project collection Helen Sutherland
collection Margaret Gardiner (illustrated)

170 *painted relief 1944–45*

collection George Gibson (U.S.A.)

171 *still life* (Lelant) *June 14–47*

collection Lefevre Gallery

172 *project 1946*

collection National Gallery
New South Wales, Australia

(Alice through looking-glass)

173 *still life 1946*

174 *still life 1947*

Lelant, Cornwall 1946
175

176 *Portreath, summer—45* collection David Baxandall

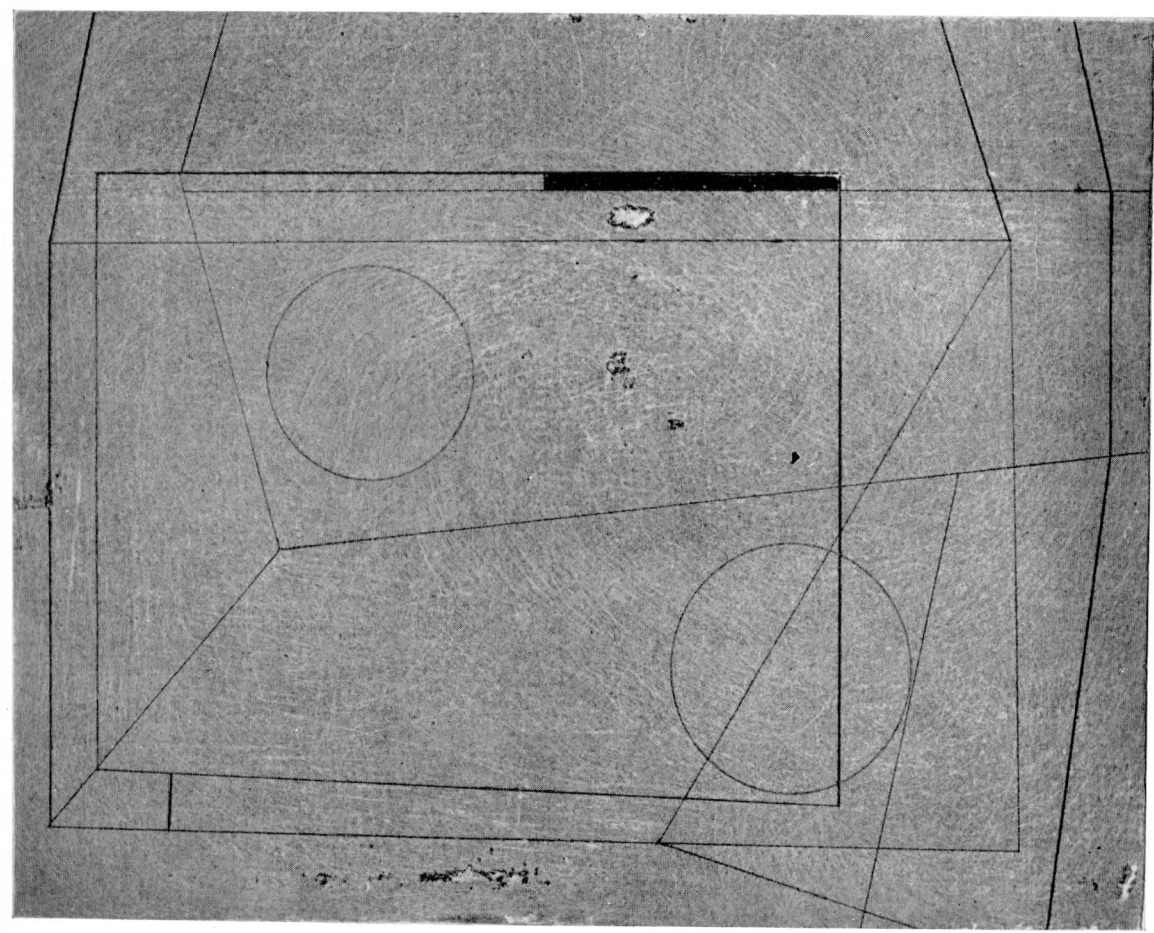

177 *Trendrine, summer—47*   *private collection U.S.A.*

178 *fives, February 12—47*

179 *still life* (*spotted curtain*) *March 14—47*   collection Aberdeen Art Gallery

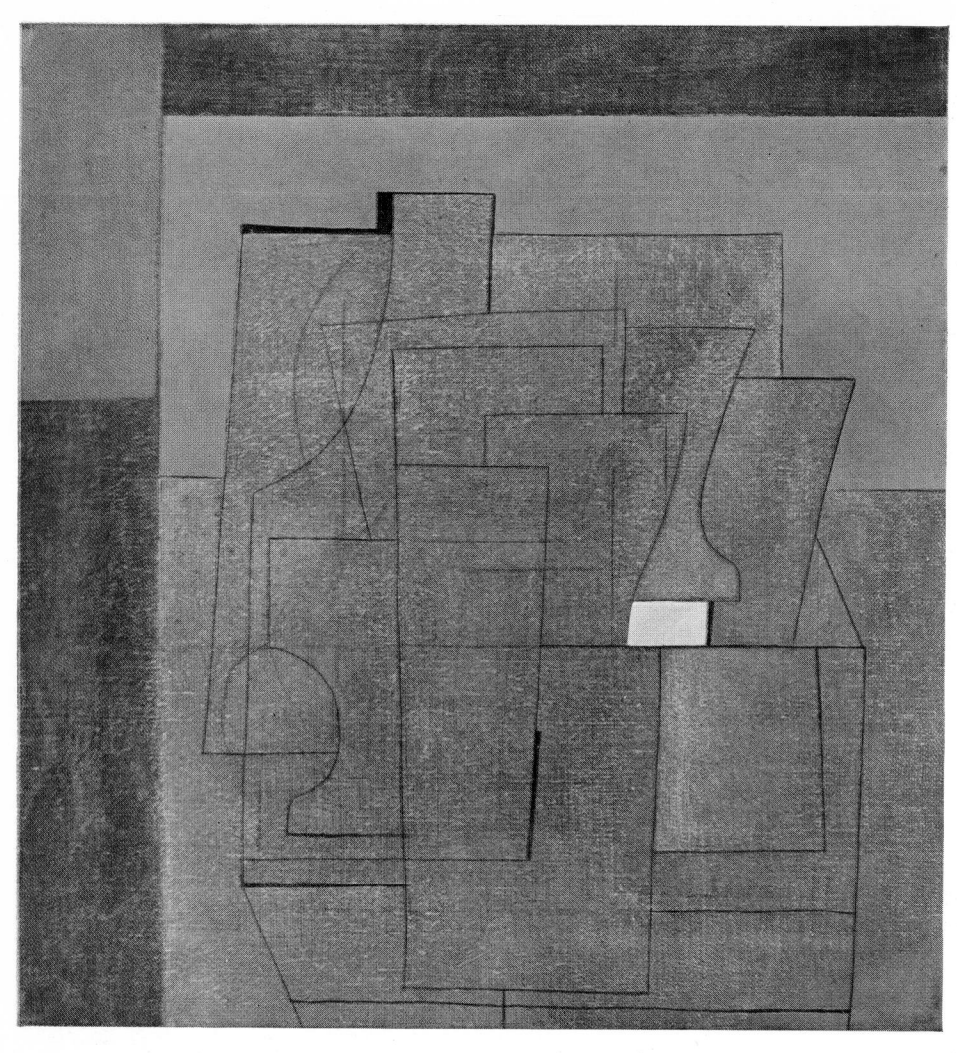

collection John C. W. Dix (U.S.A.

180 *still life* (poisonous green) *1947*

collection The British Council

Mousehole, November 11—47

181

collection Phillips Gallery, Washington

182 *Trevega 1946*

project (illustrated) collection E. C. Gregory
large version   collection S. Kaye

project for two forms 1946–7

183

184 *still life* (*winter landscape*) *1946*   collection C. S. Reddihough

185 *painting* *1944–45* version 1   collection Lily Macdonald (illustrated)
version 2   (midget) collection Aase Vibe-Hastrup
version 3   (midget) collection Warnett Kennedy

186 *still life* (Odyssey) July 25—47

187 *Lelant, summer—47*

188 *still life November 25–46*

189 *painting 1945*

collection Kenneth Clark

190 *foxy June 15—47*

collection C. Kearley

191 *still life* (cerulean) *1946*

192 *still life* (oval theme) *July 8—47* collection Kenneth Clark

Newlyn, summer—47

193

collection C. S. Reddihough

Mousehole,
summer—47

194

(destroyed)

195 *painting* (yellow and violet on brown) *February 5—47*

collection Manchester City Art Gallery

Mount's Bay, summer—47

196

197 *project* (pyramid), *March—47*   collection L. Y. Baker

198 *still life* (Odyssey 1) *July 22—47*   collection The British Council

199

painted relief (West Penwith) *November 23—46*

200 *painting* (J.L.M.) *February 2—47*

201 *Trendrine* (2) *December 13–47*

November–47

still life (brown and green)

202

203 *still life* (rhino) *March 13—47*   collection F. L. S. Murray